IMPROPER
BEHAVIOR

ALSO BY ELIZABETH JANEWAY

FICTION
The Walsh Girls, 1943
Daisy Kenyon, 1945
The Question of Gregory, 1949
Leaving Home, 1953
The Third Choice, 1959
Accident, 1964

BOOKS FOR CHILDREN
The Vikings, 1951
The Early Days of the Automobile, 1956
Angry Kate, 1963
Ivanov Seven, 1967

NONFICTION
Man's World, Woman's Place: A Study in Social Mythology, 1971
Between Myth and Morning: Women Awakening, 1974
Powers of the Weak, 1980
Cross Sections: From a Decade of Change, 1982

EDITED BY ELIZABETH JANEWAY
Women: Their Changing Role, 1972

IMPROPER BEHAVIOR

Elizabeth Janeway

WILLIAM MORROW AND COMPANY, INC.
NEW YORK

Library of Congress Cataloging-in-Publication Data

Janeway, Elizabeth.
   Improper behavior.

   1. Conduct of life.   I. Title.
BJ1581.2.J37   1987   303.3   87-1545
ISBN 0-688-04897-8

Printed in the United States of America

First Edition

1   2   3   4   5   6   7   8   9   10

BOOK DESIGN BY DALE COTTON

This book is dedicated to
all the kind friends
who wrote me warm and interesting letters
to which I failed to reply
while I was writing it.

I hope this study of "improper behavior"
will atone for my practice of it.

Contents

Chapter 1

"DOCTOR, I DON'T FEEL WELL,"

says the worried patient. "I have trouble getting to sleep and my digestion bothers me too. Then last week I developed this terrible rash ..." Or words to that effect. You can go on, I can go on. "Doctor," we all say sometime, "I don't feel well. What's the matter with me?"

Here is someone looking for a definition. What's the label that will identify this irritating collection of ills that has cropped up to plague you or me, him or her? We've run into unexpected trouble. We badly need to understand what we're up against. We want this mysterious invasion of coughs or headaches or lower back pain sorted out for us, named and defined. But how, in the everyday world, do we define "defining"?

In general we expect definitions to give us more than names. Suppose that the doctor were to answer our question literally: "What's the matter with you? Oh, I'll be glad to tell you that. You've got shingles [or measles, or chicken pox or AIDS]. If that's all you wanted, you can pick up your bill from the nurse as you leave." We wouldn't like it at all. That wasn't what we meant!

In general, it seems, we expect definitions to tell us not only what is, but what to do about it; to show us how the world fits together and how its different parts connect and work. In this book I am asking how *definitions* work, beginning with the odd fact that when we ask for a label we are really asking for the right way to deal with some disruption of life's normal course. A label isn't a cure, after all, and we really know that perfectly well. Yet that's where we often start. What do we expect to get from a name? What's the power of naming?

Once upon a time there were clear answers to that question. Names themselves could be magic. To raise up a spirit by spells, for evil or good, one had to summon it by its proper name. Today we don't ask the doctor for magic spells but we still want him to use a power that we don't have, his expertise. The flavor of enchantment that lingers in naming, works subconsciously but still powerfully to give us help. If your back pain or my cough can be identified and labeled, certain things follow.

For one thing, the illness is really there. You and I, he and she, are not kidding ourselves if the doctor declares that, yes indeed, we are suffering from kidney stones, ulcers, malaria, or conjunctivitis. We don't exactly welcome the news but it does place a nameable disease on a medical map. An anonymous disorder suggests a different sort of label and it's an ominous one. No one likes to admit that "they don't seem to know what it is." Anxious friends nod sadly at such disclosures and talk with embarrassed optimism about consulting specialists, or new tests that they have read about in the newspapers. If the doctor can't say what an ailment is, it might be anything and we fear the worst.

Second and more important, placing our trouble on a medical map implies that the doctor knows what to do about it. A label is the first step toward action. Doctors can't prescribe treatment till they know what they're treating, and since we're the ones to be treated, we very much want them to know all they can. The treatment may not be pleasant and we know very well that we can put up with discomfort best if we can trust the expertise of the authority who puts us through it. The doctor knows what to do, we say to ourselves.

When the doctor doesn't, we're not happy. Second only to the anxiety that goes with an anonymous ailment is the risky submission to life as a guinea pig. "I want to run another test," says the doctor, and the heart of the patient sinks. What kind of an expert keeps on experimenting that way? we ask testily. We want the security of believing that our experts are sure of their ground. Then we're ready to face our adversary-illness and endure the part we must play in the campaign for health, where we serve as both foot soldier and battlefield.

Of course if we were to think about it with complete objectivity, we might recall uneasily, in the watches of the night, that over the centuries earlier generations of doctors, along with wisewomen and medicine men, have diagnosed a wild variety of symptom patterns, placed them with assurance on maps long since discarded as quaint examples of primitive illogic, and gone on to treat these erstwhile diseases according to systems of cause and effect that run the gamut of human imagination. People like us who didn't feel well, couldn't sleep, had a terrible rash, have been physicked by shamans and bonesetters, have been cupped and purged and bled, dosed and poulticed, subjected to icy baths and electric shocks, injected, braced, kneaded and punctured, exorcised, immobilized, starved and intoxicated, hypnotized, tied down for the convenience of barber-surgeons, prayed over by priests in the suffocating smoke of sacred fires and counseled by astrologers—all with a magnificent diversity of results. Sometimes these patients died of the disease and sometimes they died of the treatment. Sometimes they survived, sometimes they actually felt better when the virus or the doctor wore out and gave up. But almost always they put up with it. So do we.

Why? Why do we seek out the experts and beg them for rules and prescriptions when things go wrong? Why are we so sure that such directions for proper behavior will solve our problems and cure our ailments even when the behavior prescribed turns out to be inconvenient, unpleasant, and painful? Why do we demand structures of definitions that can harden into cages and prison cells?

It's our need for maps. They deliver us from chaos: medical maps that give the doctor leave to function and the patient leave to hope that these evil-tasting medicines will work; moral maps that filter our reactions to the outer world into segments marked "good and reasonable" or "highly dubious"; maps of learning that assure us of truth and falsehood and fearlessly place one statement on this side of the dividing line and another over there; maps of status and hierarchy and entitlement that lay out our rights and justify our demands; maps of time that fit rumbustious daily events into historical processes; and other maps of time in the shape of calendars that sprinkle our weeks with days of work and days of rest and our years with ceremonies; maps of the universe; maps of heaven and earth, maps that lay out proper relations among classes and races and genders and castes; maps of music or dissonance, tones and modes; maps of dance that give meaning to gesture; maps that show museum curators what pictures to hang where—in short, maps that place us in the world whenever we need to know who, what, or where we are.

For how could we know, without them, that we even lived in a world shared by others who use the same rules, a world governed according to familiar instructions? What definitions do for us is to establish exactly this mapped society, labeled and described and knowable. A solitary universe in which nothing we encountered had a ready-made name, a universe that would have to be invented and charted by one soul alone in the space between the galaxies, that's what the terrified mind conceives it would face if our maps were to vanish. Terror of the nameless is what gives the power to define its overwhelming authority.

That's what we want when we go to the doctor with troubling questions. We want his expert knowledge, but we want comfort too, the comforting knowledge that we aren't alone with our worries. We individual humans are social animals as well. In confusion and distress our minds reach out for one another just as our bodies huddle together in one another's warmth.

But of course we are alone, since we social animals are also individual humans. Comfort isn't enough; we want to cope with our misery, end our sleepless nights, and we turn to our maps for help. They aren't just static descriptions of the world; we look to them for directions and prognostications. Let these definitions mutate into prescriptions! So our need slides into belief that needs will be answered and our maps will show us how to reach our goals, win friends, find a lover, a career and fame, get rid of that awful itch and sleep all night. After all, it's these maps that have named the constellations, charted the earth and sea, planted cities and set up hierarchies of power. Surely they can tell us what to do; or at least the experts can read them and tell us.

In a perfect world we could leave it at that. Proper behavior, prescribed by some learned sage, would guide us safely to a happy ending. But a perfect society would have to be changeless, static, since any change would make it less than perfect, and not even the most traditional cycle of Cathay has ever been that. All of a sudden familiar landscapes can be rocked by earthquakes or devastated by floods. Invaders from the desert break through the Great Walls that authority has built, or a merchant class pushes its way up into the ranks of the aristocracy. Wars destroy established elites, and interstate highways do the same for the scenes of our childhood. Our old maps of behavior are discredited and out-of-date. Things have to be redefined, put together in new patterns that will include some entities we've never seen before.

Most change is not that dramatic, of course. But, slow or fast, redefining maps is a continuing necessity. Whose job is it? Authority claims the right, and it has a lot on its side, its label tells us so. But established authority is stuck with its own traditions, which shaped the old maps, and they are now definable as the problem not the solution.

13

This situation is familiar in any time of transition, like our own. A great many matters are up for redefinition; perhaps authority itself and its standard prescriptions are threatened. Can it keep control of its ability to define the world of reality in which we live, and do it well enough for us to accept its maps and prescriptions and trust its colleges of experts? Only time will tell, but as we wait for an answer, we can follow the players best if we understand the rules of the game. It's these rules that I want to investigate here. I want to consider authority and examine, most particularly, its great and neglected asset—the power to define. How does it work, what does it intend to do, how does it fall down on the job when it fails? What are the tools it uses to convince us that authority knows what it's doing and that we should go along? As you can see, this book is full of questions in pursuit of answers, which they will not accept easily.

Defining authority means looking at what it does not include. Those excluded from power make up two groups. First there are the general run-of-the-mill rest of us, ordinary citizens, who want simply to go about our business and are happy to have authority's maps to guide us. But there is another set of folk who find themselves in opposition, though not all of them have chosen to be there. Aside from the visible dissidents who have their own programs and know what they're for as well as what they're against, many bewildered people are buffeted by amorphous forces of rejection and denial in an undirected, half-conscious rebellion against the maps that describe the right way to see the world and to act within it.

Authority calls that improper behavior and has a number of labels to attach to it: criminality, deviance, dissidence, or just bad manners. Once it's employed the label, authority is apt to think it has this outburst of disorder under control. Sometimes that's true but often it's not, and the reason is that the label doesn't always apply: It has no relation to the rest of us do. Dispelling doubt therefore looms a bit larger for the experts, and they feel a need to reinforce their prescriptions by increasing our faith in them. The methods they use are instructive. They turn up in many other situations. Enhancing our trust in their treatment is held to be therapeutic in itself, and therefore justified because it enlists the patient's will to get well. Well, hope, though hardly scientific, is pleasanter than despair. We listen and hope, even if we occasionally wonder about the patients who hoped but didn't get well.

Certainly hopeful patients will trust the orders they must follow more readily than suspicious ones, and a very good way to reinforce trust is by involving the patient in active participation in the treatment: We identify with the treatment and believe in its usefulness because we are part of it. We down our medicine, go in for exercise or cut it out, give up liquor or sweets and confront an array of tablets and capsules on the breakfast table, and the very act of abstaining or doing confirms our part in a common enterprise. Doctor and patient become partners. Our involvement supports our belief in what's being done *to* us, because we are, in part, doing it ourselves; and we wouldn't do it (would we?) if we didn't think it would help. Our trust may waver in time but as long as we go on following the prescriptions we're given we haven't abandoned our last shred of faith.

My mother's father was a homeopathic physician and though he died before I was born, family loyalty made sure that the illnesses of my childhood received homeopathic therapy. Let me tell you, it kept the patient occupied. A glass of water, faintly colored, faintly bitter, stood on the table by the bed and the patient was directed to take a teaspoonful *every fifteen minutes* while in a waking state. No one in the care of a homeopath could ignore the efforts being made in the name of curing. The doctor was trying, the malady was truly engaged. It was hard, therefore, to doubt the definition of the problem when it gave rise to such persistent activity.

In other times and other places stronger drugs, nastier

This approach is so taken for granted that any failure or gap in procedure makes us very uneasy. We bear our troubles best if we know (or think we know) their origin. For that, they must be not only identified but *identifiable*. They must be recognizable; and that means that they must have happened before, must already carry a label. A single event leaps from the stream of time, but if it can't be recognized, it vanishes back into mystery. Elusive happenings posit no maps. They're useless for understanding the present, plumbing the past, or predicting the future. They're glitches and gremlins that wink and grimace and disappear without offering pointers for action. Before we can name them we have to see them again; and again . . .

The power to name, say the fairy tales (remember Rumpelstiltskin), offers the hope of controlling events by identifying the pattern they fit into. Alone, they are unknowable and therefore beyond our hopes of control. When we ask for a name, at the doctor's, we are asking for a pattern too. Our troubles may seem to us to be uniquely pressing and painful, but the last thing we want is for them to be unique in themselves, for then no one would know what to do about them. Doubt like that is worse than knowledge of doom. When the AIDS epidemic was young, not only were fake cures for AIDS peddled at high prices, so were fake tests to discover its presence. "What's wrong?" we dare to ask because we need, so much, a plan for action.

If, in the doctor's office, we know that we need prescriptions, we don't always know it in other situations. That's too bad, for if we think all we want is a label, we may be satisfied, or at least silenced, when that's all we get. Here we come—worried, polite and tentative, asking for information about what's wrong with us or with the world—and we're told that that's the way things work and there's no way to change it. Sorry, says authority, but there's nothing to do about this distasteful bit of reality you've stubbed your toe on, you'll have to live with it. We get a diagnosis that says no cure exists. "Life is unfair," says authority, "but we never promised you a rose garden. You'll just have to make the best of it." And maybe authority is right, but how seldom we ask it, or ourselves, whether it might not be mistaken.

Perhaps we would do that more readily if we realized that "There's nothing to do about it" is also a prescription. It points the disappointed questioner to a special kind of action: Grin and bear it. But bearing pain, injustice, fraud, and all the slings and arrows of outrageous fortune is not an invitation to relax. Sitting still in the face of humiliation, mustering active psychic restraint to stop the natural urge to cry out in pain, scratch that infernal itch, explode in fury at the frustrations of living as an underdog, that's action, prescribed action that is not intended to cure our troubles. It certainly is a guide to proper behavior, but not for the benefit of the patient, not to help us cope with problems, but for the convenience of others including that of authority. If we disobey, here come the labels that name us deviants, rebels, outlaws, criminals, or crazy people.

That's one sort of unsatisfactory answer that the power to define can supply, an answer that stops too soon. Another sort of unwelcome answer gives us more than we expected. The treatment prescribed may be what is called heroic with the patient as astonished hero. Doctors, having been granted authority over the physical self for therapeutic purposes, consequently possess enormous power to interfere with that self. In the name of expertise and good intentions they are held immune to laws that would prohibit such invasion to anyone else. They can spray us with X rays, shift our moods with drugs, dull our reasoning powers, turn us yellow, bald, totally insensitive, and cut into our unconscious flesh. Our hope of cure and our needy dependence on their expertise wins our informed consent no matter how small may be the information we command. Their ancestor shamans can have had no greater basis for doing no less to our feverish ancestor patients huddled in the smoke of sacred fires and drunk on peyote or soma.

Do not imagine that I am denying a human need for doctors and doctoring. Clearly the role of curer is necessary to society and always has been. Who among us would prefer to suffer alone, without comfort and help and without the directions that promise to lead us back to the ordinary world that seems so delectable when we're banned from it? No, I want simply to examine the way that the power to define operates, and the responses that it intends to call forth. The medical map is a useful example because, one way or another, we've all wandered on to it sometime and have found ourselves wrestling with its experts and definers in situations that are extremely important, at least to us. At the same time, we know they can't be as important to the doctor in spite of the purpose we share. Here the line between agent and patient is clear and so is the need to commit ourselves to proper behavior, as laid down by the expert. The power we bring to the relationship seems small. We can grumble, we can ask questions that obviously can't be drawn from experience or training that matches the doctor's, but if we really get crosswise with this authority figure, our only recourse is not very effective improper behavior: We can't do much more than leave. Malpractice suits? Well—do we really want to experience malpractice?

Of course, we may be sure that we have run into malpractice and then, yes, indeed, we want to sue. Rest assured, our experts will find that improper behavior of the worst kind. But though it may appease our anger in a particular case, are we going to spend the rest of our lives undoctored? Unless we do, we will find ourselves back in the same patient/agent relationship again, asking questions of another expert.

The familiar example of doctor and patient, that is, can stand for many situations in which authority has to be consulted by unauthoritative us, ordinary folk, who may certainly be experts in some field, or even in medicine, for doctors do ask each other for treatment, after all. But there's a background to this example, and the more we wonder about what we're told, the more the background attracts our attention. There is, we begin to see, a more misty power that lies not with the experts but with the rest of us, and that is the power to accept one expert, or one kind of expertise, over another, to pin our faith to this map instead of that one.

There is also the power to decide, in some general, societal fashion, that a particular field of activity has identified itself and become recognizable until now it demands a set of experts to consult along with institutes that will grant them the certificates of expertise that will enlist our belief in their power. Consider, for example, the increase in the number of business schools granting degrees at undergraduate and graduate levels in the last twenty years. A hundred and fifty years ago, it was divinity schools that flourished. It wasn't our advisers who set this process in motion. It was a response to feelings of need, to recognition by us advisees that we wanted someone to answer new questions, to draw us relevant maps. "If God did not exist," said Voltaire, "it would be necessary to invent him." What agent could undertake such an invention, if not society at large, all of us anxious human beings? As far as God is concerned, a number of people, including Voltaire (though he was careful in his language), have believed that this is exactly what we did. If we could do that, we could surely invent doctors to service our wants, professors and expert magi of all sorts.

Is authority, then, not a charismatic inborn strength blooming in sages and leaders through the force of Nature informed by Divine Will, but a gift to the powerful from the rest of us, out of our need? Does our longing for wisdom and for guides through a wilderness world drive us to create an ear, human or sacred, to hear us and a voice to answer our cries for help with comfort and counsel when we have to ask, "What's wrong? What shall I do now?" Debates over the origins of authority are probably as old as humanity and certainly as old as written records. They are made more complex by the fact that if authority is to be of any use to us, it must have the power to declare its primacy—convincingly, too.

But if it were truly absolutely primal and authentic, would it have to convince us? Would we even have to ask? Would we feel a *need* to ask?

In an earlier book, *Powers of the Weak,* I explored what seemed to me to be the techniques for asking and arguing, and for action by the governed majority, in the face of the edicts and directions of constituted authority. I tried to exclude consideration of the powers of the powerful because they have been discussed since time immemorial. But I could not help running into the willingness of the rest of us to accept the subterranean force of definitions. Most of the time both governors and governed, definers and the directed, assented to whatever explanatory schema was put forward by the society they inhabited, whether or not it seemed to contradict their own interests. When a woman ran for vice-president in 1984, some other women were greatly distressed. "I don't like it," one told a *New York Times* reporter. "We aren't meant to be politicians." "Why not?" the reporter did *not ask, or at least she didn't report it. The original answer, which cited the rules f*or female behavior in public, was a sufficiently clear response. Readers could be trusted to understand it.

What I want to understand is something different: How do we arrive at consensus? Why do we accept the rules that, as above, may seem to contradict our own potential for doing, our own self-esteem? What psychological mechanisms are at work to promote our everyday taking-for-granted of rules? And equally, what is going on when we stop taking them for granted? For Geraldine Ferraro's nomination declared that not every male or female human being believes, today, that women aren't meant to be politicians. A map is changing, has already changed considerably. It will influence other patterns of behavior. How does this come about? What makes breaking rules first possible, and then acceptable, and then commonplace? There is a tension between authority and the rest of us, it seems, which surfaces first in behavior, not in ideological, intellectual disagreement and argument.

Back to the doctor's office for a quick illustration. I remember once challenging medical expertise without in the least meaning to. How well I recall the ominous response, as from the heights of Olympus (and indeed I was in the New York institution named Mount Sinai), when I observed to a doctor that I was suffering from bronchitis. To me, that was merely a helpful bit of data indicating a very sore throat, but authority took it as usurpation of its prerogative to name and to prescribe. "I will tell you what you are suffering from," it said brusquely.

I was, I remember, too taken aback to apologize. I certainly hadn't meant to encroach on a medical map where I didn't belong. I was as convinced as anyone that the doctor knew more than I, that I needed his expertise. I hadn't been questioning his authority, for anyone in trouble wants not just any old answer, but a really authoritative answer. Why should he feel a simple remark was so inappropriate? Why should the medical profession need to guard its status, keep its distance, from the other half of the relationship so imperiously? We are, I was, quite willing to take his special wisdom for granted, why else was I there? Why else does anyone come to consult the oracle? We know we need definitions and prescriptions. And yet . . .

Chapter 2

AND YET THERE ARE SURPRISES

that accompany even the most authoritative and the most sought after answers. As we've seen, the advice from experts may tell us there's nothing to do and give us no comfort at all, only counsel that's painful to follow; or it may prescribe treatment that, as far as discomfort goes, is worse than the disease.

Even more disconcerting is being told that we've imagined ourselves onto the wrong map. "What's the matter with me?" we ask the medical doctor, and are referred to another authority entirely. It's not the physical self that needs attention but the mental or the spiritual being. Or, vice versa, we consult a counselor for help in dealing with depression or with mental confusion and find that psychic anguish is laid to physical causes. We had been contending, we thought, with high questions of philosophy and ethics or with the very ground of existence, and then, to our dismay, these problems are attributed to deviations in bodily functioning. Our hormonal levels have got out of whack just as if they were the four humors that were held by our ignorant unscientific ancestors to govern the body's well-being, and the doubts and the visions they've occasioned are to be treated with Valium or lithium salts or electric shock.

Or again, now as ever, another great system of belief may hold out another map declaring that the contagion we've caught is sin. Why not try God? ask the apostles who accost us in the street or airport with good news, or the voices in the air that speak revelations through the television tube.

Conditioned by training and constrained by need to look for experts and maps, we find that there's a plethora of maps around, and they disagree.

That's hardly news. Creeds and causal systems have argued with each other for millennia, and even so we and our ancestors have managed to live in a world of differing opinions. Philosophical disputes don't often affect the price of fish or wine. Yes, we say to ourselves, in the upper reaches of theory, where Plato argues with the Sophists and Hegel with Kant, maps no doubt disagree, and even our familiar proverbs seldom convince us that what's sauce for the goose is entirely acceptable as sauce for the gander. But unless the argument hits us where we live and disrupts daily life, who cares? Let the professors and pundits enjoy themselves with learned disputation; it's another attribute of the experts that sets them off from the rest of us. It may even be useful if it keeps their minds sharp and ready to supply the answers we want.

And yet. There are. Surprises. Philosophic discussions can harden into theological battles, and disagreement can escalate until it is given a new label: heresy. And heresy leads to crusades. Then religious war lays waste the land and terrorists bomb ordinary citizens. Cities are made desolate, children and old men starve, women sharpen knives, boys and girls throw stones at the occupying troops or blow up passing buses. Opinions have become matters of life and death, witches are burned and dissidents tortured, and contending authority is better avoided than sought out. It won't just give us an answer that may or may not be useful; it will demand that we demonstrate our agreement on pain of pain.

Our Western society seems particularly prone to disagreement; or perhaps we simply know enough about it to pick up on disputes when they happen. Still, more slowly changing cultures do probably manage to match up their disparate maps with greater ease than we have done. At some times in some places, it's been taken for granted that illness was the natural result of violating religious law by breaking a taboo, while flouting custom and morals was often met with shouted public disapproval and harassment. Things have been different with us, at least from the time when Job received a diversity of advice from sympathetic friends, or when Apollonian reason confronted Dionysian frenzy. When the infrastructure of life is solid these differences don't interfere too much with daily existence, but they are always potentially present as a threat to order. Offering answers that can't be reconciled, they leave questioners at a loss; that is, without a trustable map.

We are beset by such disputes today. Is juvenile crime evidence of natural wickedness (original sin, our great-grandparents would have said), or of a breakdown in family values, or of social stress arising from speeded-up processes of urbanization and neighborhood decay, or is it perhaps due to the low value currently placed on unskilled labor and the high rate of unemployment among young people that inevitably results? May a good man who is also gay use his insights to counsel other people or must he be barred as a sinner? Can a loving lesbian mother raise a "normal" child? Is abortion murder or a medical procedure that should be readily available to women hard-pressed by unwanted pregnancy, in a society that declares families sacred but offers little practical support to them? Authority is ready to answer, contradicting itself or sometimes simply saying, "Shut up. Go away."

We can't blame authority alone for that reaction if we believe that it is a construct that has developed to serve the rest of us, to answer our questions and help us manage existence in all its complexity. We have had a hand, if only by our acceptance, in sanctioning the argumentative maps and the bickering pundits. Argue they may but even if authoritative directives do no more than harden our will to confront our problems, that's better than abandoning us to despair. Indeed these disputes serve to emphasize the centrality of the issues being debated, their importance to the community of which we are a part and the value of shared communal life itself. The maps tell us we're not alone, others have been here, some have survived; maybe if we adjust the directives of authority a bit we too can do that. If we have too many arguing authority structures, each reflects a need that required its plan for action, and maybe each is useful in its own way or own sphere, where it fits our questions more coherently than any overall pattern could. If a neat, complete social map of the total system seems intellectually satisfying—well, pluralism has its own advantages. It's surely better to have a chance to disagree with the Moral Majority or the Communist party or the mullahs or the medieval Church than to have none, not only for dissidents but for society at large. Pluralism promotes both flexibility and diversity. Even Mao Tse-tung once opined that letting a thousand flowers bloom was a good idea.

But obviously if we choose pluralism, as we have, we have to expect surprises when we pick the wrong pundit, when we get disagreeable answers, or conflicting advice. The problem we know about has begotten a problem we did not expect: how to tell the right expert from the inadequate or irrelevant wrong one. *That question is not one we can trust pundits to answer.* Practically speaking, their authority may be great in the field they know, but outside it they are as ignorant as the rest of us. "That's not my century," a historian told me once in answer to a question about a slightly later time; and though I was surprised (Wasn't she interested in the roots of her period's events? Didn't she want to know what happened next?), I did come to honor her for her honesty.

For when maps disagree and experts fall to arguing, it isn't facts that are in question, but interpretations of them. Any bits of data may be true, but the question is, Into what pattern do they fit? Unless we know that, we can't get sailing directions from them. Unfortunately we usually prefer to talk about, argue about, matters that we know are there,

that we can go out and kick—statistics, personal evidence
that can be clearly put into words; but these things aren't always there in full "thereness." One man's teapot is another
man's kettle, one woman's career is another's dereliction of
female duty to home and family. Or, instead of different
labels for the same event or activity, the same label will have
different meanings for different people.

A couple of years ago, Senators Helms and Hatch set
the Congress plus a vast crew of expert witnesses (each with a
map) debating the question, "When does life begin?" Facts
flew like hail but they only raised more questions: "How do
you define life?" "What do you mean, begin?" Nobody could
catch those flying facts and settle them neatly onto one chart
whose relevance could be agreed on. The same data supported discordant conclusions based on incompatible premises. As time passed it became clear that the only sensible
question to put to the disputants was, "Why are you asking
this question?" The senators, it appeared, were not looking
for a way to cure a social problem, but instead for a problem
that could be defined in a way that suited the treatment they
had in mind to supply.

They had an answer. What they wanted was a question
that would fit the map they favored and prescribe the action
they wished to see taken: to deny the right to abortion on
moral grounds, refuse to consider the social causes of unplanned pregnancy, and shun as immoral the pragmatic deterrent to abortion that easy access to contraceptives would
provide. Turn a blind eye to another possible deterrent—effective social support that would include practical job training for single mothers. Create a climate in which the rights of
future citizens, the born children, would loom as large as
those of the unborn. The opponents of the militant anti-
abortionists, well aware of the purposes and the agenda of
the other side, entered the debate waving their own maps as
if they were battle standards. Since everyone was committed
in advance to a contending answer, the debate was clearly

not an exploration of facts in order to shape guidelines for action, but a contest of political clout.

There's nothing wrong with such contests as long as the debaters and the audience don't fool themselves about what's going on. A pluralistic democracy does indeed have to settle some disputes by furious confrontation. But in such contests, the facts fall out. They are reduced to references advanced to support different philosophies of life. They cannot, by themselves, provide guidelines to appropriate action.

Just the same in cases like this, action may still be necessary, experts or no. That's when the untutored rest of us have to step out into an extra dimension, the uncharted space surrounding our maps, and choose between the definitions and directives they offer; or if none that exists is relevant we may have to set about creating a new structure for interpreting recalcitrant data in order to resolve the problems that caused the hullabaloo in the first place. In these cases the expertise of the experts may hurt more than it helps for it can offer no innovative ideas. It has fitted the data together into a mosaic that can't be shifted without being destroyed.

Finding that oracles advise conflicting courses is a common enough experience in everyday life. The evening paper's astrologer doesn't often agree with the one in the morning paper. If our problems aren't very pressing, we may simply go with the counsel that pleases us most. The crunch comes when we're up against a decision that matters and have to settle on a course of action that may have serious consequences. Shall we gamble by acting on our own? Shall we consult, let us say, one financial analyst and move on to another if he or she goes wrong, with the option of trying still a third? Not only are we plagued by lack of confidence in ourselves: Comparing analysts may very well diminish our wholehearted faith in expertise itself when some of the pundits turn out to be no wiser than we are. Whom can we trust? we ask. These fellows are nearly as bad as politicians. As Alexander Pope put it, "When doctors disagree, who shall decide?"

Now as then, it appears, the answer can only be, "The patient decides among disputing doctors," for there's no place else to turn unless we are willing to trust ourselves to chance entirely. Some of us do, or think we do; but even for the most fatalistic, a rationale by which one superstition is referred to another often crops up: The casinos are full of gamblers with systems, and players of numbers don't choose the ones they favor at random. Putting oneself in the hands of fate may seem like a decision to give up deciding, but it is actually the choice of a different map with a different kind of causality, drawn from the tarot deck perhaps, or the *I Ching.*

Whatever our choice, what we decide is not which doctor, or map, is *right,* for how could we know that, lacking expertise? What we decide is, rather, which doctor we *trust.* Like gamblers without a system, our choice is made in the realm of indeterminate possibility, where an infinity of futures lie waiting. What we have to judge isn't facts but coherence, convincingness, plausibility, the human feel of the doctor's counsel.

"Believe what's plausible," seems tautologous as an approach to definition, to say nothing of being unscientific. But humankind acts that way, just as it accepts a doctor's prescription because the chance of cure seems better if you follow it than if you don't. In fact, humankind is not as ignorant as it may think. We've had more experience evaluating different courses of action than we may realize if we see them formally as major, cogitated decisions. Making this choice instead of that is something we've been doing all our lives. Those schools of business administration that we've decided we want have elevated decision-making to an academic discipline, to be studied scientifically, or at least in an orderly way. Nothing wrong with that, as long as the exercise doesn't separate making choices in a formal setting from making them as an everyday activity, involving informal interpretation and intuitive selection. Man cannot live by logic alone, nor woman either, if logic leaves out relevant human experience, conscious and unconscious memories of what has worked before, and, in addition, the whole weight of the question under consideration: How important is this decision? What commitment will I, will others, be making to it? If I am seeking a counselor or analyst or spouse — how much of my life am I investing in the answer? When we have to decide between two courses of action, two contradictory sets of advice, it's neither expertise nor formal logic that rules in the end. It's general wisdom.

Part of that general wisdom, which must acknowledge the commitment that has to be made, must also pay attention to the needs of the decider. We do read the astrologer (if we read any) whose predictions seem to address our own concerns. When we consult the experts, it is *we* who are present, *our* problems we are asking about; and we want those we question to consider the significance to us of the troubles we bring to them. If questions are important to us, then that's part of the context in which they have to be answered, whether they seem important to the doctor or not. We need to understand, and to be understood. Nor are we wrong to feel that doctors and prophets who pay no mind to the plausibility of their responses are distinctly insensitive to the immediate context of reality, which includes the patient. Perhaps the proper prescription is so commonplace that describing it is boring, perhaps it's so new that it's risky, if not dubious, but the patient still wants to be put in the picture in which, after all, he or she is a central feature.

Plausibility appeals to our judgment of the world based on experience and tested by earlier decisions. The word may seem to give too much weight to the persuasiveness of arguments made for a particular recommendation, but how persuasive they are in the end is really up to the listener. If we invent another term, a new label, which might be "logical coherence," then we're inviting our own sense of discrimination to get into the act. Does this argument hang together? Is it self-contradictory? Does it ignore some fundamental things we know about life and events and procedures and causality? That is very much part of the great tradition of scientific thought, and I was interested to find Douglas Hofstadter discussing the matter in a column in the *Scientific American*. He was talking about the claims of "marginal science" to belief, reports of UFOs, of telekinesis, of prevision, all of them "improper" by the standards of normal science but quite impossible to disprove by marshaling facts.

"What is under debate," Hofstadter wrote,

> ... is in essence the nature of correct arguments. What should be accepted and what should not. ... [These are] not easy questions. ... They involve a paradox, a tangle in which ideas being evaluated are also the ideas doing the evaluating. The only recourse is to common sense, that rock bottom basis of all rationality. Unfortunately we have no foolproof algorithm to uniquely characterize that deepest layer of rationality, nor are we likely to come up with one soon. For now the core of rationality must depend on inscrutables: the simple, the elegant, the intuitive. This paradox has existed throughout intellectual history, but in our information rich time it seems particularly troublesome.[1]

Hofstadter, something of a definer himself, is speaking to the troubles felt by experts when some variant events, hitherto unexplained, are pulled together into a novel identity and are demanding their place on a map. Can they be admitted? Standard answers aren't enough. Plenty of scientific discoveries have overthrown old maps in our culture, and just because a hypothesis doesn't fit is no reason to label it false. The earth goes around the sun, the atom can be split, in spite of the views of our ancestors. How, then, can we tell fruitful hypotheses from interesting theories based on misreading of events, on discovering patterns that turn out to be accidental, or just on towering imagination?

Hofstadter tells us that what we have to rely on, finally, is "common sense, that rock bottom basis of all rationality." As he says, it is not simply rational in the sense of being logically reasonable. It includes "inscrutables: the simple, the elegant, the intuitive." *These qualities shape and govern aesthetic judgment.* They enter in the service of creativity, and the use he asks of them here is to decide when creativity has skidded off the track and is pointing in the wrong direction. But creativity is a vital component of all action that deals with changing reality, reality that has to be seen with fresh eyes. Our present-day culture seems to think of creativity as mainly confined to a special kind of expert: to artists, writers, musicians, and the scientists of new breakthrough concepts. It's nowhere near that special or that rare; it is very much a part of daily life. It is flexibility, adaptability; it lies in questions rather than in answers. It is the raw material for new definitions and new maps, a universal ingredient of learning. We use it all the time when we ask ourselves if a neighbor or a fellow worker is telling us lies, if the boss will really fight to get us a raise he's promised, or whether our true love is true. These are aesthetic questions. We get the answer not by rote, but from the experience that has shaped itself into our personal maps of the world as we expect it to be.

From our own experience, that is, but also from our awareness of the experience of others—we humans who are individuals and social animals, too. We find our way not only from maps, but from what happens when their advice is implemented. The doctor's prescription must be carried out by the patient, and it's the patient who will know whether the medicine works or the regime is helpful. The petitioner to the oracle either follows its counsel or does not. If not, the counsel becomes moot; if so, then the result is known and judged by the questioner, not the oracle. And when politicians disagree, their constituencies may reelect them enthusiastically, or they may not. "We"—the patients and petitioners and governed—we are always present. The map makers must check from time to time to be sure that the outlines they have drawn fit our experience closely enough for us to go on accepting them as accurate: They must be plausible.

If the maps no longer fit, how long will we use them? Our own creativity will begin to ask questions as the errors pile up, and if our questions aren't heard, then we won't be able to follow the advice that doesn't fit our hopes and needs. Improper behavior will be seen, by authority, to occur more and more frequently, more and more egregiously. Our own native powers of definition are beginning to unmake the old maps that we can no longer trust.

Chapter 3

"ALICE, WHAT IS THE ANSWER?"

said Gertrude Stein on her deathbed, or so the story goes. "I don't know the answer," Alice Toklas replied. A silence. "Then what is the question?" asked Stein, and died.

Mythic or true, the anecdote sums up a life of questioning rules, and of improper behavior. It's plausible, a likely story. In itself it has also become a touchstone for our uncertain age. When answers fail, we do look for new questions with which to confront our lives. Often they are as misty and numinous as Stein's, for in order to find new ground to build on, they must reach outside of time and off the map, any map. Just because they are so hazy, authority can dismiss them, at least in the beginning. "How can you expect to get a sensible answer if you ask silly questions?" says the rational power to define.

Well, there you are: How did we know the question was silly? And must we agree that it is? Why should we believe the label that definition slaps on it unless there is a real power concealed here, anxious to persuade us that authority knows best? We like the Stein story, I think, because it challenges the whole idea that only exact answers count and that only precise questions, the ones designed to produce exact answers, are worth listening to. Can it really be that the world is made up of little pebbles of information, each of them fitting a particular slot of a question? Is there nothing else to be asked? We know better than that, and in Stein's question we hear a voice speaking from the space that surrounds all the maps, a voice that suggests that our own tentative gropings after meaning may be more central to understanding the world and ourselves than any cut-and-dried logic. If there's more to life than we have ever known (and how can we imagine that there isn't?) it must be at once familiar and mysterious, lying within and without consciousness in some yet to be discovered form. We need questions large enough, powerful enough, as a scientific hypothesis is powerful, to break old rules of asking.

Naturally the old rules resist. Stein and the rest of the avant-garde of the early twentieth century were laughed at as foolish and condemned as outrageous at the same time: Her work was a mélange of "silly questions," said respectability. She played irritating games with syntax and words as a kind of tease. If she was really trying to tell her readers something new and important, why didn't she do it simply and straightforwardly, so that people could understand what she wanted to say? Why tie it up in knots by insisting on breaking rules that served other writers perfectly well?

That reaction is a perennial problem for unconventional thinkers and creators in any medium. How can you communicate your thoughts or demonstrate your hypotheses by conventional means when all the values and standards that you want to challenge are built into those means? Science and new technology today like to declare that they encourage "lateral thinking," new ways of seeing and putting data together—but all systems have an inbuilt resistance to what has not been programmed into them through the premises on which their rules are based. Even the most welcoming areas of innovation can handle only so much of speculation. "What is the question?" is a fine and necessary question, but it ought to receive some response before more unforeseen queries arrive to muddy the already foaming waters.

It is rather as if people asking such questions (misty and numinous) find that they are looking for general rules about discovering general rules. We must ask again, "How do we define defining? What is it that we try to do when we wrestle with the shapelessness of life-off-the-map? How do we judge the worth of one question against another?" Hofstadter's "common sense . . . inscrutables: the simple, the elegant, the intuitive" supplies a good answer, but it's not a final one. How does common sense deal with avant-garde work? How do we *recognize* simplicity and elegance combined in a way that we've never seen before? I recall walking through the Museum of Modern Art in New York some years ago with a young person who remarked, "I like this [Jackson Pollack painting] better than that one." I realized as he spoke that I was not capable of saying more about his preferred work of art than "That is a painting by Jackson Pollack." I could recognize, but not discriminate. Before I was able to do that, an extended act of looking had to take place. It has now been done. Thirty years later, walking through the same museum with the child of that child, I was able to agree when she said, in her father's exact words, "I like this one better than that." My eyes, habituated to other patterns of art, needed time to learn critical judgment.

Our acceptance of definitions, then, depends on their fit with what we know from our experience. We can, of course, enlarge and deepen our experience; look at avant-garde (as it was then) painting for a generation, and see into it better. Such acts, however, require our participation. Unless we involve ourselves in looking (or listening, or reading, or steady repeated activities) we don't learn to judge new elements in reality. And if we can't judge for ourselves, we may more readily go along with the definitions and prescriptions that authority hands us, but they won't mean much. Most of the time, our indifferent agreement will be all that authority wants; but not always. In times of stress the strength of any group depends on contributions, of ideas and inventive insights and work and commitment, from its ordinary members. These things are the active side of loyalty. If definitions move toward prescriptions, and prescriptions toward action, the governed who have been told what to do become, in fact, implementers of decisions. How good will they be at that?

How deeply committed will they feel? How easily can they monitor the directions given them and shift them about if they are not working well? For the best directions don't run just one way. They depend on feedback from the staff of workers who are out in contact with reality. All effective action is in some sense a partnership.

But it isn't easy for authority to see either the presence or the value of the lower ranks, who must be convinced that their directions are practical and the definitions they're based on are plausible. If you look up the word *definition* in the *Oxford English Dictionary*, what you will read is "A precise statement of the essential nature of a thing." Well! What more does that say to the lower ranks than, "Shape up! We're telling it like it is! Don't argue with essential nature!" But when one takes that definition down into daily life, it needs a few words added. I'd rewrite it to say, "A statement, as precise as conditions permit, of the essential nature of a thing as it is perceived at the time by the people examining it." My amendment is clumsy and qualified, but it brings in the perceiving human beings who have to be persuaded to come up with a consensus on what is plausible in terms of their lived experience before they can *do* anything with the term in question. There's a kind of creative shiftiness in definitions, it seems, that they themselves, like authority, don't want to admit. By insisting on their ability to discern the "essential nature" of anything needing definition, they attempt to raise plausibility to the stature of absolute truth; and thus define themselves, by implication, as being beyond questioning.

Happily there's an ordinary human "commonsense" component built into applying definitions and prescriptions to reality that necessarily confronts them with questions. When the lower ranks start implementing orders, they are very likely to find gaps in them. You can tell people what to do, but they may discover that you have not told them how to do it. "What's the best way to follow the rules?" is a perfectly natural question, but if it doesn't get answered sensibly it can be a prelude to querying the rules. Improper behavior, asking awkward questions, may be the result of a heartfelt desire to do one's best. When in doubt we all want to penetrate beyond the letter of the law to the purpose of the spirit. But whose interpretation will we accept most readily? Yours? Mine? Theirs? The intent of the Founding Fathers as they wrote the Constitution? We won't avoid questions that way.

Can we learn something by going back "to the beginning"? But what beginning? The realm of platonic ideas and essential natures would like us to believe that it never began but existed a priori before and outside time and process.

That statement may be definable as myth or as philosophy, but it will never fit into the realm of dailyness where people live and make decisions; so on the whole we had probably better pass it by and consider our own humble personal beginnings. The premises that explain the world and set out the rules to run it come to us early, and we ache with desire to understand the workings of reality and our connections to them. How do we draw the limits between the interior, experiencing self and the astonishing world around us? During the last century an enormous amount of energy and creative perception has gone into studying questions concerning early childhood development. How does experience shape and become a coherent personal self? Different terms are used by different students but throughout there is a sense of a process by which perceptions are tested by activity and woven together into a system that both describes and explains outside reality and develops an individual person who is a functioning part of the world, an agent as well as a registrant of experience, the two processes working together.

It's rather as if each human creature grew up in the middle of an enormously complicated reciprocating engine, experiencing sensations and perceptions and putting them together into a series of connected hypotheses in order to cope with these demands and impingements. Child grows, experience shifts and broadens, and a new system forms. The need to deal with the outside, intruding continuum calls up a respondent interior continuum, a person with a memory, who can say, "This has happened before!" and go on to learn "When it happens again, look out for this to happen next." Remembering the past tells us what to expect from the future. Events and sensations recur and can be recognized; some recur more often and can be defined as "permanent." They come together in patterns, and patterns shift the meaning of the individual events by relating them to each other. Permanence does not have to be static.

The psychologist Jean Piaget speaks of "accommodation" and "assimilation" as the self adjusts to reality and then adjusts its image of reality to changed expectations. Erik Erikson sees each human creature as going through stages of growth that carry lessons and inculcate the virtues central to the surrounding culture. The work of these two child psychologists is old enough to take for granted a vision of culture that is not only male-dominated but patriarchal in its concepts and the data they provide need to be broadened. Just the same, the idea of growth and development through interaction of person and culture, together with the ways this interaction takes place, serves as a useful guideline, which can be supplemented by factoring in other data and other points of view. Most useful (to me, at any rate) is D. W. Winnicott's notion of a continuing tension between inner and outer world, a space where imagination and creativity wrestle with reality, both shaping it and absorbing it all through our lives on the basis of early experience. All of these mental maps allow for continuing dynamic shifts in the human condition. The repetition of events and our increasingly knowledgeable responses shift what began as meaningless blips on a screen into memorable happenings that take on significance as they come together into patterns. Out of these relationships appears a consistent view, held by a coherent viewer.

At the deepest level of self-knowledge and world-knowledge, our sanity itself depends on our capacity to note and remember, to name and set in relevant patterns the blips on the screen that we identify as messages. Unless we learn how to learn, we're stuck where we start. Contemporary psychological research suggests that if we can't put data together, form connections, and work out distinctions among entities and people and processes and events, the possible person that each might be is caught in chaos and disarray. Without the glue of memory, grains of experience don't come together. Maps and patterns don't take shape and grow into systems of thought that match our interior world to what's outside, including the worlds that belong to other people. Common experience, known to be common, permits communications and shared movement, and what is shared is the similarity of patterns—maps.

But a shared recognition of data isn't all that growing and learning brings us, not by a long shot. Our bits of fact arrive, are remembered, and shape themselves into patterns in an aura of emotion. As Descartes remarked, our thoughts assure us that a thinking self exists to house and observe them. But they aren't observed coldly, they are *felt*. It's feeling that makes us pick out this or that blip on the screen and remember it, watch for it *before* we know its name, long for a label that will help to fit it into a pattern. Oh, childhood agonies and ecstasies! Oh, spirit of Saint Sigmund, pointing grimly to the hidden existence of events that arrived in so painful a fashion that memory looked away and let them be hidden in the depths, where they could not be retrieved and dealt with actively—and consequently have shaken our lives with volcanic spasms ever since! Our maps only look flat. In fact, they are multidimensional.

By the time we're old enough to worry about such things, we have all acquired a self that is mentally present but also uncertain, prideful, and terribly anxious to know how to cope with what's going on. We've made our dynamic maps and they in turn have made us, though never finally.

But the ways of making and of changing remain those that we learned when the first outlines and patterns were formed by the children we used to be, that race of little people born into the power of giants, whose language had to be taken in, whose ideas had to be divined, whose emotions shook us and whose plans and goals we shared and also struggled against as we encountered and doubted the lessons and virtues of maturity. Children don't learn, nor do parental giants teach, in abstract serenity. Loving, longing to please, rebelling in rage, frustrated and hopeful, fearing and dreaming of freedom, we work to record and then to reshape an internal landscape of the mind; a landscape that endures to guide us when our adult selves come to face dilemmas in a world that can shiver and shift in the twinkling of an eye.

At the beginning, when our first lessons in labeling were confirming our acquaintance with the world, inner feelings and outer reality were as close as they could be. "That's the baby's nose," says the baby's mother, touching what she names. "Here's the mommy's nose," and touches her own. "That's the baby's chin." And so on. "Shoe, shoe," she says. "Here's the baby's shoe. We put on the baby's shoe." "Shoe!" says the child enthusiastically, delighting in a new-found power to name, linked to action, to what it's proper to do with a shoe. Would the baby learn faster if her own nose, her mother's nose, were not the entities being labeled and touched? Of course not. Her awareness of her existence is intensified by knowledge brought home to her own personal self. Reality out there is touchable and knowable; it pertains to her.

But the labels declare that they aren't just personal to her, but symbolic of categories of things and conditions: *baby's* nose, *baby's* chin, baby's *nose*, mother's *nose*. They identify a class of things and they endure in relationships. Permanent and personal, they confirm the child's permanence as a personality that endures in an enduring and recognizable world. In learning names, she confirms herself as a naming person who lives in a nameable world. As she does so, she learns the means of naming and recognizing again: a language that endures, is hers, and refers to what's out there. The recurrence of events, the appearance and reappearance of things that have names attached, the permanence and patterning of life, all come together to establish the realness and "thereness" of world and of self.

As time passes, these parent-child interchanges cease to go just one way. Children learn that names can be used not just for statements but for questions too. In some societies, like our own, adults deliberately, if unconsciously, invite questions by asking and answering them even before children have the words to do it themselves. "What would you like? The ball? Here's the ball. Would you like to throw it back to me?" Action, as here with "throwing," is often invited, no doubt because it lets children confirm understanding without words; but even if it isn't specifically suggested, the activity of asking is. Learning is a dialogue, they learn. You can take a part, you don't have to sit and wait to be told. You can enlarge your own maps.

New patterns and linkages and depth of detail, these grow too. A six-year-old knows her nose and can go on to draw a face and give it a label: It's a mean face, it's happy, it's a cat's face, it's Uncle Ben. A nose isn't an isolated feature, it belongs with eyes and mouth, and the face it fits has an expression. We move from data to patterns to meaning.

It isn't always easy. There's a distance between first recognition and taken-for-granted assurance that what you see is what others see. A part of the meaning of events is something that adults seldom teach explicitly, and that's the *importance* of any entity or condition or action. Wary and uncertain, eager for praise, children want very much to know not only names and patterns but how seriously they are expected to take them. If things need names, so do our feelings about them. "Is it all right for me to feel this way," children need to know, "or have I misunderstood what it means? Is it all right for me to cry because I feel so bad"—here is the action connection again— "or will I be teased for it?"

These are hard questions to ask, and the abstract quality of definitions, the dictionary message about "essential nature," doesn't make it any easier: How does my essence know that it's feeling the way your essence does? Children who draw "a mean face" have been given a label but not an explanation. They have felt a hurt or been scolded for meanness without knowing just what went wrong. Where did the mistake come? If you don't know, you don't know how *not* to do it again. Doing it again, of course, is one way of asking for explanations, but not a very pleasant one. It's apt to be treated as willful improper behavior. Pictures can be questions too. A cat's face may be asking about the mystery of animal life, alive and willful but not like us. How important is the difference? Is teasing the cat as bad as hitting your brother? Uncle Ben may be a favorite or very much not, or he may be queerly, confusingly, absurd (read: different), so that drawing his face asks about the proper behavior of adults, how much children can learn that is trustworthy, and from whom.

The abstract nature of definitions is a screen against hard questions. What can one do about the essential nature of something? Obviously one can't hope to change it; one can only go away, leave it all alone, and accept that the matter defined is settled and inarguable. Happiness is always delightful; meanness is always vile. No use to protest that Uncle Ben's present was not that enchanting, or that you didn't mean to be mean, someone else started it. These are childish excuses. "You must learn better," says the power to define. And sometimes we do.

For yes, oh yes, we do want to know what it's right to feel and to do, how to behave, what to pay attention to, and yes, oh yes, we learn a lot by going wrong and being scolded. So much of what goes on in the mind of the guardian giants who raise the young is mysterious! Children proceed by hard listening and inspired guesses and, when that fails, by asking the sort of questions that adults find hard to answer, the ones that start with "Why?" but don't fit into any adult map of causality: "Why is the sky blue, Mommy?"

In the adult world the blueness of the sky is important only sporadically, if a trip to the beach or a picnic, say, is being considered, or if rain will disrupt a ceremony or a baseball game. As an abstract inquiry it doesn't connect with any general agenda for action, and therefore has no special importance. Some kind of well-meaning, more or less accurate explanation, remembered from a science course, may come to mind, but when you offer it to the child it's evident that question and answer don't meet head on. To start on what you recall of how the atmosphere scatters one wavelength of light and lets another through is clearly not responsive, and you'll lose the attention of your dear toddler before you reach the end of your sentence. But what you have done is answer the hidden question, Is the blueness of sky important? You have made it clear that nobody cares.

Suppose it was important. Suppose the myths of your tribe declared that all would be well under this cerulean arch, that Mother Goddess Earth would bring forth fruit, that the Lord God would withhold his wrath, that the serpent eating the universe wouldn't get around to eating us for a while—unless the clouds came over, the heavens opened, the Ark foundered, and blueness was gone forever. Do that, and your child would pay attention. Add a little hellfire, inculcate the rules for proper behavior through repeated rituals and celebrations (actions) ordained by authority, and the blueness of the sky takes on considerable weight. It speaks of some Mighty Being, a Lord God who can order the universe, and disorder it too; call forth blue skies and green earth, snow, ice and rain, dirt and earthworms, animal life . . . Everyday existence takes on a new dimension if it exists as if by the prescription of a willful deity and can be changed by the fiat of same.

Power like that is important, and not just in the abstract. If the way things are arranged right here, where the child lives, is thus controlled, then disputing the rightness of what's out there means disputing the will of some Immensely Powerful Force. The blueness of the sky merges into the idea of an authority that not only knows and defines but *enforces* a right way to behave and believe: Whatever is, is right and, what's more, is inevitable. Accept definitions, then, don't tangle with the Essential Nature of the Lord God, don't ask silly questions, and do as you're told.

Of course as time passes and the serpent goes quietly on eating another part of the universe and the dark star, Nemesis, refrains from hurling comets at the earth, the normal surprises of life will raise some doubts about inevitability and the total, universal rightness of what is; but the connection can linger on underground. If we reject the map that our parental guardian giants took so seriously, we may still want one that lays down other laws as forcefully as the old one did. Even though we grow a bit skeptical, we need a connected world view whether or not it shifts a bit from time to time. We need the definitions that have been put together out of accumulated human experience even if their essential nature is subject to slippage. We want cookbooks and dictionaries, manuals of etiquette, road maps and advice on how to succeed, get thin, survive divorce or find a new lover. What they tell us gives us a start on action.

But let's not forget the questions that have evoked these answers, or the long process of adjustment and assimilation, of imagining a world and testing that image and shifting it and wondering still how important are all the things we know, and what we have overlooked. Let us be willing to go on asking questions that don't fit patterns. They are humanity's defense against standard answers that rise like a stockade around authority's citadel and would have us believe that all is known, that prescribed behavior is the only correct behavior, that the doctor knows best and will cure our ailments if we simply obey and take our medicine. For when push comes to shove, we don't in fact act like that We question and doubt and misbehave.

Chapter 4

IN THE DOUBLE HELIX
OF QUESTION AND ANSWER

new ideas and unforeseen events tug at the structure ordained by authority, and authority struggles to control the solutions these challenges demand. In fact, it would like to do more: to control not only the answers but to direct or to censor the questions asked by limiting their range and their nature. If queries can be called awkward or inappropriate they won't be launched so easily. Label them as improper behavior and their value will be minimized while the questioners who foolishly raise such matters can be isolated from potential allies. There are a lot of plausible ways to do this and we will look at some. In general, however, can we identify the map that authority uses when it's determined to resist unwelcome challengers? Are we, for example, students in search of directives, asking only to be instructed in the ways of the world?

We may think so, but authority doesn't. Its name for this map is "politics." That label comes naturally to authority, whose primary purpose is to stay in charge of the world, or at least in charge of as much of the world as it can manage. Standard political practice has a lot of familiar rules, but if we are not aware that we're playing that game, we can be quite surprised when we find them applied to what we imagined were innocent questions. Raise a point that puzzles you, and discover that you've taken on the identity of a challenger. The tactics roll out to cut you down to size. "Divide and rule," mutters authority to itself, and sets out to isolate the questioner. After all, the more complete the division and the smaller the resulting groups, the less any group can hope to accomplish; and the optimum-minimum group, of course, is one person. A solitary individual can be shoved right off the public map of politics and any awkward questions attributed to personal problems: He had a terrible childhood. She's a lesbian, you know. There's a criminal strain in that family. Then breaking rules turns into an individual singularity and won't be seen as a general attack on authority's management of affairs.

In itself, naming a map "political" can have a deterrent effect, for politics has got itself defined, one way or another, as being "dirty business." Ordinary citizens, hearing that label, aren't eager to get tangled in the meshes of politics, a reaction that leaves authority in charge. But *all* dynamic relationships are political to some degree. Managing any kind of affair involves groups of people that operate in much the same way. Authority may like to claim primacy for its ideas, but public matters are resolved, in the end, by a process of bargaining. Let's say that push comes to shove. Opposing interests make their arguments, perhaps on television, perhaps in front of smaller audiences, in boardrooms or cabinet meetings or university committees, and try to gain support. Ideally any disagreement would be settled once and for all in a single decisive confrontation. But usually disputes end in compromises, more or less enduring, more or less livable for those concerned. When they come apart as new stresses demand adjustment, the whole process starts up again. True believers may well declare that such bargains are corrupt, but like all definitions, that of corruption changes its specifics with time, class, or culture.

Of course dirty business may be a factor in any compromise. Bribes and blackmail are effective ways to arrive at agreement on common action, for a while anyway. They can shut up potential questioners, at least those who are subject to pressure. But let the compromise stop being livable (and the mere passage of time can do that), and someone, perhaps a new political player or a newly organized group with its own interests, is going to start wondering about its utility. Even more likely, a collection of someones will start acting in ways that are unexpected; difficult to handle; improper. This compromise, it's clear, has got to be renegotiated. More dirty business? Perhaps. But what Freud named the reality principle is going to intervene with annoying insistence until its demands are satisfied.

So true believers can't count on principles, enshrined on moral maps, to win the total victory any more than the corruptionists can rely absolutely on money and blackmail. No matter how convinced people may be of the nobility of their goals, an announcement to that effect is not likely to gain the immediate consent of their opponents. Like everyone else, crusaders must argue, bargain, and persuade the rest of us, not just that their purposes are *pure*, but that they have some value for nonbelievers. In fact the utility of exchanging quid pro quo isn't hard to discover. A moral majority quickly learns how to stage dramatic demonstrations of their tenets, rename and redefine people and things and activities, declare their convictions unchangeable, and then retreat a step or two until they end by accepting some bargain or other on the grounds that of course this is not their final position. "Not your final position?" their opponents may say. "You don't expect to abide by the bargain you made? You call that *moral?*" They do. It's an effective political stance.

People break rules, it seems, for many reasons. Crusaders do it as a matter of principle; even when they use the rules, they regard them as supporting an iniquitous system. Members of an avant-garde, like Gertrude Stein and her contemporaries, are eager to call attention to the limits of the old maps. Both groups, however, are well on their way to becoming a conscious, differentiated center with its own different set of rules. In the beginning, when a label of improper behavior can be most disconcerting to the one so named, people often break rules without intending to: because rules hurt, prevent action, deny hope, and neglect hard cases.

If they didn't do that they wouldn't be rules, which must always stretch averages toward the condition of universals. As long as the averages on which rules are based remain average *enough*, the rules are challenged only incidentally, and "average" appears to blend into "normal." What's expected can be defined as what is right, and that's comfortable all around; everyone would rather be right than wrong. But in times of change, anomalies increase and averages find themselves sustained by slimmer and slimmer pluralities. Rules hurt more often and more severely until the limitations they put on activities become crippling. The hard cases that they have ignored increase until they become a majority.

Then the rules go through a metamorphosis, a change in nature. They start to be seen as more trouble than they're worth, and though moral prescriptions for behavior may hang on for a while, behavior itself pays less and less attention. Consider the ancient rule that forbade sex out of wedlock for young females. It was, in my youth, under some pressure to change but there were still pejorative labels for rule breakers. "Damaged goods" was one that we city sophisticates laughed at, but it undoubtedly carried weight in other areas. And indeed there were solid grounds for holding to the old rules. The limericks that mocked them laid out substantial reasons for proper conduct: A wayward young woman might well fear the consequences of improper behavior; "babies, and Jesus, and social diseases" were not to be taken lightly.

These same eventualities exist today but the significant judgments attached to them have altered and the old rules have all but lost their plausibility. They have not so much changed as faded away. Rules for manners and etiquette and for proper dress for particular functions have dimmed in the same way. The maps that once illustrated them are still to be found and they are still ready to answer questions, but who now asks these questions? They are no longer relevant to what we want to know. Rule breakers too have disappeared, in the sense that they are now no longer defined as challengers to a system. The system, with all its framework for directing moral and social traffic, has faded into the background and we simply get on without it.

This kind of disappearance of systems and maps is, in the main, a healthy response to change. Society loses some special virtues and some valued roles, but sustaining them in the face of changed conditions is very costly. And the good old days don't stay good if they have to be propped up by sacrifice and artificial manners. Indeed any major change in the social and/or economic structure can only be halted by all-out efforts of denial, rejection, and the outright falsification of actual events in the interest of "saving the hypothesis." Such concentration on preserving a status quo that has started to slip wastes energy that's needed elsewhere. Nonetheless these desperate confrontations happen because old roles and positions are so emotionally charged that losing them seems to promise catastrophe.

History has a lot to tell us about class conflict and race conflict and religious commitment, but the unresolved change that we are caught up in today is unique in its depth and scope and, therefore, in the number of rules that are being challenged and broken. The trouble that results is defined and labeled in any number of ways by any number of groups. It provokes passionate opinions and deeply ambivalent feelings, multitudinous accusations, and, no doubt, many secret confessions of guilt, plus a welter of contradictory directions about how to deal with it. I'm talking, of course, about the changing position of women and all that goes with it: the economic and social effects of work outside the home instead of in it, for money instead of for love (which is slang for "free"), shifts in gender relationships and nonshifts in overall male/female income differentials, and the disruption of traditional family patterns. Let us not overlook, either, the community's responsibility for family support, an ancient custom that seems to come as a stunning revelation to many, even to those who extol it as a part of the neighborly world of our ancestors.

Since these troubled topics have been debated by thousands (including myself) over the last twenty years, I am anxious to focus here on the specific modes by which authority and the power to define grapple, in this continuing struggle, with rule challengers and rule breakers. We have come a long way from the individual example at the start of this book, in which a patient with a problem is looking for help from an expert in labeling and prescribing for illness, to a tumultuous and rowdy carnival of naming and unnaming, of deconstructing maps and altering significance of symbols. Trying to understand the language of change, vocabulary, grammar and syntax too, by leaping into the middle of a gladiatorial contest-cum-circus is an extreme form of total immersion. On the other hand, that's where we are in daily life, immersed in a kaleidoscope of data. We have little to lose by confronting the maelstrom.

In fact the center of our contentious confusion is exactly a matter of definition: What is the essential nature of woman? Answers fly up in a swarm, as if we'd opened Pandora's box, and perhaps we have: Woman is best defined by her unique ability to bear children, an ability that is taken to imply the duty of raising them. Thus she influences the future through those to whom she imparts the vital moral values of her culture, society, race, nation, and class—or what have you. No, says another voice, woman is primarily human and is female only as a qualification of her generic humanity. Like men, she can define her life's task as being, in Freud's words, "to work and to love." Like them, she can move beyond the home and family. She may even enter those higher spheres of power where Man ruled alone for so long.

At this point in the argument, however, one begins to hear a definable female voice start asking some elementary pragmatic questions dear to the heart of that other Freudian vision, the reality principle (who must, I feel, be a goddess, not a god). "But will I get paid the same wages for my work?" she wants to know. "Can I hope for the same honors? Virginia Woolf's procession of 'sons of educated men'—bishops, judges, admirals, generals, professors, and doctors—has become more open to female marchers than it was in her own time when the daughters of educated men came 'trapesing along at the tail end.'[1] But when am I going to march at the head as easily as my brothers can? Will the same number of distinguished scholars praise my work in the same tone and words as they use for my male colleagues? When I run for political office will campaign contributions pour in as readily as they do for my brothers? And above all, what and who will give me a hand with the work that still has to be done back in my old place, the living space that was labeled the domestic sphere at the point in history when it profited the men to go out and work somewhere else, in factories and counting houses, when making goods for sale left the home workshop and left us women behind there?

"Does the work that I do define me?" the voice continues. "Or does my essential nature, whatever it is, prescribe the work that I do? Am I or am I not a person within myself, blessed and lumbered with free will, with choices and obligations and responsibilities like all those other human creatures whose selves and roles are held to be normal because they were born with external sex organs, instead of having them neatly tucked inside, like my mother and sisters and me? And why, for heaven's sake, is their position so important?"

As you can see, my spokeswoman—and she's only one out of a myriad, all of whom might voice their questions in different forms—still looks at our world in terms of present definitions; and why not? A need to redraw maps and to renegotiate bargains has to be carried out in action—political action—before the definitions that derive from authority—and which legitimize authority—actually change.

Our present definitions are still based on male experience. Eveyone, male or female, learns them young and they stay with us at least until the bargaining starts. It's unlikely, however, that even a temporary truce that redefines "the essential nature of women" is going to be reached until female experience gets into the process. And of course female experience and its value is exactly what the argument is about. This argument, then, is particularly hard because it's dealing with two things at once, both the subject and the methods that are acceptable as validating contentious statements. No wonder that both sides wish, from time to time, that the bargaining might stop!

A growing sense that revaluing male experience is also necessary doesn't make the dispute any easier, either. After all, a duty to rule and define the world, including the argumentative other half of the human race, must have influenced male values profoundly in the direction of seeing dominance, even oppression, as an unavoidable obligation. No wonder that the masculine party finds that an unpleasant way to describe its past labors! Responsibility is a much nicer word.

Meanwhile the old agreement on gender relations is coming apart at the seams. I've no intention of trying to unravel the whole tangle, but a look at one particular area of difficulty can illustrate the problems of, and the need for, redefining proper behavior. Let's take the old view of women as being private persons.

The label fits into the tendency for the power to define to isolate dissidents. If you are a private person, any problems you run into are private too; they are personal dilemmas that have to be faced and solved all by your own lonely self. Our culture has traditionally held women to be private people whose official dealings with society at large should be mediated by male relatives, an identification that ended not much over a century ago; both my own grandmothers, in fact, were born into this situation. The system that forbade the public, political participation of women is gone so thoroughly that it seems an ancient irrelevance, but prescriptions for behavior are still influenced by the principle that mothers belong in families. Economic necessity, of course, may drive them into the outside world, of work-for-money, but until recently this regrettable situation was held to be the only acceptable reason for female involvement in public activity. Even so, if competition with men followed on employment outside the home, the inner virtues so essential to mothering—love, patience, and self-sacrifice—were thought likely to be violated. And indeed bringing up children does impose different rules for interaction from those taken to be suitable in the world of work, though the real question is whether these rules should be gender-linked.

Today mothers at work outside the home are a large majority of mothers, but statistical data don't wipe out definitions. If your integral, inner self is properly labeled "mother," then mothering is not just a job you do but the primary job you do and a chief identification. In a pinch, job or career is generally expected to take second place. Where that expectation does not hold, a conscious determination to reject it is almost always necessary. In any case, discovering who is going to share the duties and joys of bringing up your children is a problem.

At the moment two general solutions to finding help in child raising exist. Since they are distinctly related to money and to class, that also complicates matters. The first is to hire someone else, a trustworthy surrogate nurturer, to come into your home; which means that if she has children, she will have to leave them in order to look after yours. That decision pushes the problem one step away but it doesn't solve it in principle. *Some* mother can be defined as neglecting her duty.

The other solution is public rather than private, but note that *thinking about it still remains private*. You as a mother must still decide whether to hire a "homemaker" (if you can afford it) or to look for child care outside the home. If you believe that mothering is the label that defines you as a person, you may well see yourself as shunning your duty and behaving most improperly if you opt for child care, no matter whether money forces the decision or not. Your worries will double if you doubt the reliability, or even the safety, of the choices available. Revelations of sexual abuse of children in some centers and nursery schools have nourished a bumper crop of anxiety and guilt. My point: *It is still private guilt. Child care is your responsibility and yours alone. It is not, as you see it, a community obligation, not something due a public person whose obligations serve society as a whole.* And yet these children you're raising are the next generation of citizens who will make up the community, shape society, and meet its obligations. In so doing, all parents undertake a social task.

It would be wonderful if someone could provide a sensible answer to this huge and disabling problem; but when we phrase the dilemma that way we are asking the wrong kind of question. Who raises the children is of course a private matter; the decision will be made by individuals. But it's a political question too. The contemporary need for child care arises from changes in society that are not the result of personal choices, while the effects of inadequate family support are public too. But the difficulty won't be handled until the need mothers have for other adults to help in the important job of child raising is seen so clearly that it can be bargained out as a public matter and an acceptable arrangement can be devised for dealing with it. As I write, we are still improvising; and the rise in the cost of insurance for child-care centers is aggravating the problem

Here again the mere existence of an argument over the nature of women hinders solutions. If women can't sort out their primary duties, can't define their own inner selves, why should the rest of the human race get into the dispute? How can they, if the self-definitions necessary for judgments aren't there? Another of Freud's touchstone remarks is the famous question, "What do women want?" Female indecision also marks us as being private people, inexperienced in the area

57

where public, political decisions are made. Male judgments, based on male experience, operate here, whether for good or for ill. Women are seen as novices or as unfitted by nature to function in this arena, and any divergence from standard practice is therefore taken as odd. As women move into politics and the upper levels of management, they are expected to shape up and learn to replicate masculine patterns of interrelations, patterns that take dominance as the goal and confrontation as the proper instrument for gaining it. When women deny such ambitions (and a number who would call themselves feminists would do so, along with a number who wouldn't dream of claiming the label), men see it as evidence of bemusement, of immersion in a private world of dreams. "What other aims could there be?" asks patriarchal myth. The idea that other ambitions and different ways of achieving them might be conceived and used in bargaining for a less contentious world also marks women as private captives of romantic fantasy.

Privatization, then, is a powerful instrument for authority. It denies the ones so defined a place in the public world, and it therefore instructs women not to act—that is, not to act politically, as if we were fully entitled to state our needs and to work for them in the usual public fashion. Recently we've witnessed the recrudescence of a fundamental debate among women over priorities. Should we aim at a goal, equality, which is straightforwardly political and would, once gained, grant us acknowledged power? Or should we emphasize the special female needs that our nature as mothers requires? Now a problem that presents itself as a dilemma carries an unfortunate prescription: to argue instead of act. In this case, moreover, the recommendation to ask for help, if that should prevail at a given time, instructs women to behave like dependent inferiors.

But we are dependent! says the other side of the argument. We *are* inferior, in the sense that we have less power and earn less money and don't get sufficient campaign funds, or praise from scholars or promotion to upper-level jobs—

and we certainly don't get attention from the political Establishment! Doesn't the reality principle, your female goddess, justify asking for help? Didn't the fight to win an Equal Rights Amendment concentrate on the wrong goal, irritate those who would be willing to help women *as* women meet the demands of their roles, which are always going to include childbearing and some child rearing? Aren't you just accepting male goals when you go after political rights?

Well, in my opinion that argument too is going to be settled politically, some time or other, because it is a public argument about entitlements for human beings, not simply favors and assistance to women. That statement sounds like nothing but opinion, but there is more to it than that. Any petitioning group that comes to authority, asking for help, is going to be seen not just as dependent, and consequently inferior (in the eyes of the powerful), *but also as accepting the label*. Therefore any help granted, even if authority agrees that help is deserved and of overall value (that is, proper), will be defined *as a gift*.

Asking for gifts is not a good way to bargain; it's a projection of the rules of a private world into the political sphere. Once upon a time, before the Equal Rights Amendment was voted down, a woman acquaintance with a very sophisticated knowledge of both local and national politics said to me, "After we lost in the state legislature I thought we might have got it through if we'd just sat down on the steps outside and cried. They might have given it to us if we'd acted like women."

And they might have, though in that state I have strong doubts. But when would they have wanted the gift back? Let us remember a similar grant of equality to "dependent inferiors" by kindly male moralists: The Fourteenth and Fifteenth amendments to the Constitution, which guaranteed equality to black people in 1868 and 1869. How long did the bargain hold? We'll look later at the aftermath of the Civil War when we consider force as an instrument of definition; but in terms of political bargains based on gifts, all hope for black equality went into limbo in 1876, until the black power movement, demanding equality, breathed life back into the broken bargain almost a century later. In a similar fashion, public support for the needs prescribed by contemporary female roles will arrive as these needs are redefined as social entitlements, not women's special requirements.

The lingering effects of the privatization of women and of other groups who can be defined as in need of help and support, because they can't bargain effectively for themselves, show up in a label that sets pioneers in new roles and new places apart. That label is "abnormal," and it's a considerable burden to carry. It can often be presented, however, in a flattering light: "You are a very special woman who can think and act like a man. You're really different."

Try analyzing the message in that statement. First, the traditional role of women is belittled. The listener is praised for leaving it behind. She is learning the ropes, how to be like a man. But in addition, she is being invited to distance herself from other women, and to privatize herself in public, so to speak. Accept the specialness, and you find that you are isolated from your natural allies. You have *given up* quite a bit of bargaining power by that agreement to regard yourself as special.

Recent changes in programs for affirmative action illustrate how this technique is used formally. Numerical goals for incomers in work areas, intended to reverse past unfairness, are now labeled as unfair themselves. The rationale is to declare piously that any regulations that prescribe special treatment for a group are discriminatory. Instead, each candidate for advancement should be considered as an individual. Here is an inspired use of the directive for power, Divide and rule. For what's ignored is exactly the fact that the minorities and the women whose advancement was desired had *always* been perceived as belonging to groups who were out of place in *this* place. Now, all at once, the label of abnormality is removed, but its consequences aren't. Removing these consequences, one by one, as individuals are able to prove discrimination, is a good, long, boring process, illustrating another maxim for maintaining rule: Put off till tomorrow what you don't have to do today. As the old fable of King Log, who ruled by doing nothing, declares, inaction discourages rule breakers especially if they must each brave establishment prescriptions alone.

Being in a place by favor, on approval so to speak, inhibits questioning. One doesn't know the rules for asking, or how important any rule may be. As we will see in the next chapter, making mistakes in public invites discredit by shaming. The first question that my female voice out of the whirlwind asked, about equal pay, came early in the current wave of feminist engagement. It seemed to those who asked a natural enough inquiry; it can even be regarded as similar to that of the patient asking what's wrong, what can I do about my problem? In theory, at least, a free labor market should, by definition, be open to everyone with skills to sell and provide for a commensurate return to all sellers. If women were being allowed, in the 1960s and 1970s, into new fields of employment, they wanted to know how to maximize their efforts, serve where their capacities would be most welcome, and earn the deserved reward. "Why don't we get as much as men do?" they asked. What the question meant was, "How can we learn to earn equally?" What authority thought it meant was a concerted challenge to existing, proper, rules.

The answers that women got resembled those received by the children who wanted to know why the sky was blue. One sort of response provided data that were true and perfectly reasonable as explanations of the workplace but had little to do with any promises of remedial action: This was the delay response. It was pointed out that women had not been trained to skills that commanded high wages; that they had not been in the labor force long enough for many to acquire seniority; and, rather more subtly, that since they were novices there, they had not yet begun to pick up the psycho-

61

logical nuances of Getting Ahead or learned the experiential rules for presenting oneself in public as a leader. Efforts at textbooks certainly followed, but they either were, or were considered to be, very simplistic; primers for people who were never going to get very far. An M.B.A. would certify the seriousness of an incomer's desire to climb into management, but it didn't guarantee the knowledge of in-language, ways of thought, homogeneity of approach, or shared values that need not be spoken. The delay response, therefore, ran, "Wait, work, learn to do it the right way, and in time you may get somewhere. If you're really good we'll make an exception for you."

The second sort of reply took another tack and cited the intentions of the Lord God who had made the sky blue and determined the essential nature of women. It was delivered obliquely but its message was clear and familiar: "The Lord God made you female and gave you other tasks to do. If we let you through this door into our space, it will be on the understanding that you take care of that other job without bothering us about your needs. We all know you have them, though, and since they add up to your primary female job, you can't expect to aspire here, in man's world, to levels above those suitable to part-timers, transients, and migrants. How can you be expected to fly to the Coast if the baby's sick? We know you can't, so we won't promote you to where you'd have to face that dilemma."

That's a prescription for action that reads "Stop!" The doctor is telling the patient that she has unfortunately been born with a congenital defect called femaleness that will always hamper her capacities in the public arena. This diagnosis is acted out rather than being openly stated, but the old doctrine of the special spheres for men and women underlies it. If you can define women's primary obligations as being family care, you the definer can properly ignore any female requests for help in dealing with other activities because they have to be regarded as secondary.

I should apologize for making an analysis that has been made before, quite possibly to the point of boredom if not staleness. But it illustrates two not-so-stale points of definer's logic. First, when authority can name one area or set of activities as legitimate, it can refuse to take action if and when the defined person wanders into another area. Indeed, these very requests for help affirm the validity of the traditional definition. "Why should you need help unless you're in the wrong place, with the wrong job?" authority asks. "You wanted to tackle this sort of work and we were gracious enough to let you try it. Making it is your problem, not ours. If you want the rules to work for you, go back where you belong."

Second, authority can reach for plausible labels to describe anyone who challenges its rules. "Rebel" and "deviant" these we've noted. But another term can be used: "childish." Trying to do more than you can manage and then crying for help, that's not the serious, mature way to accomplish anything. It may be innocent, but it's certainly foolish, and it makes you a part of that old-women-and-children dependency.

Here is a true dilemma. "Do you mean what you say?" asks authority. Are you serious about taking on a fight to change the rules? If so, we know what to call you: dissident, crank, subversive—there's a string of unpleasant names and many of them are isolating. That's a formidable rejoinder to a simple *why* question. Many people who inquire about the way things are will draw back at once, and not just out of timidity. Women and other incomers who want to know how best to get ahead in the world of business, the professions, or government didn't mean to break any rules when they asked about unequal pay; they just wanted to know why these rules didn't appear to apply to them. What should they do? All of a sudden they were being told that they were confronting instituted authority.

Authority is always ready to permit backtracking, if

good intentions can be demonstrated. It changes its tone: Just ask your question again, politely, and accept the answer without protest. If you're asking in the right spirit, as a novice—well, as a child, since that label does fit—then we will tell you again that you have to learn the ropes, you have to adapt to the system in being, you have to realize that you're here on sufferance and actually belong somewhere else and may never, therefore, really make it here.

As soon as that's done the question becomes acceptable. *It also becomes unimportant.* The questioner is agreeing that this inquiry isn't serious because it's just personal not political, private not public. It consequently loses any subversive element that points toward innovation or different ways of doing things. And so it will receive one of those unhelpful, data-rich answers about blue sky and scatteration of sun's rays, or about seniority and skills. Alone, in a new place, unable to trust one's own experience, most questioners will accept the bargain. Given the double-bind choice, they would rather be thought of as children than as rebels.

It's not very hard to awaken the lingering child in an adult, as psychologists of all schools have been telling us for some time. We adults, powerful or lowly, experts or amateurs, learned our own identities in the years when the myths and the maps of our culture were being passed on to us, and the myths and the identities interpenetrated. We may have reached the age of discretion, or of rebellion, but authority can still remind us of a time when indeed we didn't know what we were talking about, when our activities could be rightly labeled as childish, and when we desperately wanted to learn the rules of the great adult world. Speak to us even now as if we were children still, and we will recognize the tone of voice even if we stiffen with determination not to obey. The voice invites doubts about our hopes and our purposes: *Are* we asking for the moon? One thing we learned as children was that not all dreams come true. You can't have everything you want. Some doors are really locked. Some people will never like us. The dead are truly dead. Toys that are too expensive will stay in the store window, and assuming anything else is childish. Equally, to lose your temper in the face of hard facts is childish too. We've all carried the label of child before.

So any time it's applied to us, we know its power. If dedicated activists can be renamed foolish busybodies, few followers will leap to their support and they themselves may start having second thoughts about their plans. Nursery rhymes begin to echo in adult heads. Who wants to copy the Three Wise Men of Gotham who went to sea in a leaky bowl? Or Simple Simon? Or the Three Sillies who kept hanging puddings on one another's noses till they'd used up all the wishes they'd been granted and ended where they began? Unless you are positive you can do better than that, you'd better not argue with the status quo. Rule breakers and changers need a fair degree of self-confidence to run the risk of looking foolish when they defy the maps.

Now it's also true and memorable, and a sure reason for our survival as a species, that children learn something else beside rules: faith in their own judgment, daring, pride, and enough stubborn self-esteem to stick with an iffy and unpromising task. If they didn't we'd have no risk takers or rule breakers to launch new projects in the face of stagnant rules and customs. Fairy tales and children's classics commemorate the pigheaded third son of the woodcutter who went on trying and did finally win the princess, the tricksters who got around the rules by their own crafty redefinitions, and those argumentative children like Alice who had no trouble disagreeing with Wonderland royalty and Dorothy who showed up the Wizard of Oz.

But that's not what we were taught first. First we learned (and wanted to learn) how to function in the here and now, and that meant learning the norms of society: proper behavior, manners and morals, how to make friends and to fit in with the group we belong to, how to take tests in order to move on or up, how things work wherever it is in the world that we happen to be. And the way things work is presented to us as the way they have to work, the right way. The surprises of life of course aren't absent: We learn that adults, like children, can make mistakes. But how do we know they're mistakes? Because adults tell us so. How would we know it, if they didn't? "Well, that was silly of me," says an aunt. "I should have remembered that shop was closed on Monday." Her words instruct us that she *could* be silly, but she *should* have remembered, and if we want to be not-silly, then we won't make these mistakes, we will do as adults should. What's forgivable in a child is foolish in a grown-up. Proper behavior is a sign of maturity.

And a powerful sanction reinforces the lesson: shaming. That's something we all ran into early, for it is universal to human upbringing, the curb that directs us toward propriety and is used as if it were the opposite of love. Perhaps it's only the opposite of comfort and approval, but how old do you have to be before you can sort out the difference? And perhaps shaming is understood differently by the big people who rule and raise children, as they must, experts in spite of themselves, groping for effective techniques of training. For those on the receiving end, shaming is what we never forget. Even when love or approval has nourished our growing self-confidence once more, we can still wake in the night in a sweat of torment and memory over what we once did wrong, not quite knowingly, what was judged against us as unworthy. It's easier to forgive one's own guilt than to forget one's shame.

Shame and its memory weight definitions. Shame lies at the very heart of the social controls applied to us all by the status quo. It threatens the weak certainly, but it binds the powerful too, who have so much to lose. Its use is native to a patriarchal society where the powerful define themselves as protective and responsive parents, who must at times correct their children for their own good, a society in which roles can harden until neither partner can fight free of the other.

Chapter 5

"SHAME IS A PAINFUL EMOTION,"

say the dictionaries and go on to list some occasions on which it is felt. They don't, however, try to analyze the kind of pains that cluster here. Such an analysis exists in Helen Lynd's book *On Shame and the Search for Identity,* a study that does much to map this common experience. In "shame" Lynd finds "a multifaceted word" which contrasts with "honor" as if each term stood at the opposite end of a scale of feeling about one's fitness for, and comfort in, the world as it is. Both words, she says, include the "subjective feeling of the person [involved] and the objective nature of the act" that has evoked this response. We are back in the world where children learn self-and-reality by separation, but also by connection: How, and how well, does the self match the world around? Action and its felt results are instruments of making and learning both realities, internal and external, and nothing makes this clearer than doing what's wrong, unwelcome, unexpected, misunderstood, out of place: improper.

Lynd disavows any intent of "trying to build up any logical or perhaps even consistent, definition of shame."[1] She is wary of pinning this protean emotion too neatly on a map, preferring to explore the phenomenon as it occurs in life. What feelings go into it? Can we trace the sources and follow the consequences of shaming so that we begin to understand its function? When we do, we discover that it works to confirm labels and reinforce prescriptions. "Do it this way," says shame, "or you'll be sorry."

Think first, Lynd suggests, of shame as flooding the self with a sense of *exposure*. A searchlight is turned on our privacy and what it reveals isn't just a forgivable eccentricity but a major mistake. Some silly outward error can be enlarged enormously, so that wearing the wrong kind of clothes or using a word that doesn't mean what one thought, or carrying customs into a world where they are judged vulgar or out-of-date is transformed into a symbol of fundamental miscalculation. One finds oneself confronted with an incongruous, discrepant aspect of the self that can't be hidden or denied. "We have acted on the assumption of being one kind of person living in one kind of surroundings," writes Lynd, "and unexpectedly, violently, we discover that these assumptions are false. . . . Alien people in an alien situation can see around us."[2]

Second comes the *isolation* that results from such exposure. We have set ourselves apart from the normal run of people, who know how to behave, by doing this unseemly thing without foreseeing the consequences, or realizing that we were breaking rules. Naturally we are blamed. We blame ourselves. Blame is appropriate.

But that leaves us, third, in a terrible state of *confusion*, for since we didn't know what we were doing, we don't know how to correct our mistake. We have managed to act ourselves off the maps that describe our world by doing something irretrievably out of place. At best we can try not to repeat it, but nothing will wipe out the blunder we've already made. It may be forgiven in time and even forgotten but its memory shadows the image, and the self-image, we carry vis-à-vis the world outside. "There is no clear code for shame," says Lynd.[3] It differs, that is, from *guilt*, which can be reduced or wiped out by remorse and acted-out penance so that at least a partial remedy (through action) is possible: There are prescriptions for dealing with guilt. But there is no path to pardon for shameful action. Neither doctor nor priest can show us how to remove that stain on the self.

The best they can do takes us back to ignorance and immaturity: Authority can suggest we were "not responsible" for what we did. But to be "not responsible" either labels us as crazy or lands us with the lesser, but also disabling, tag of "childishness." Lynd hypothesizes that the roots of shame may be "childish" in a specific way: The emotion may be colored by the fear of abandonment, which, psychiatrists note, can spring up in little children when they are punished for not very out-of-way misdemeanors. Is what we've done so hopelessly, stupidly bad that our parents are going to give up and disown us? And if they don't can we believe that continued loving care is what we really deserve, or is it just due to their generosity? That doubt may stir up gratitude but gratitude is not an easy emotion to sustain, especially when one is uneasy about one's own self-worth. In addition, it increases feelings of dependence on these giants who care for us, and it therefore diminishes readiness to act for oneself, to take risks and try out new adventures; they might go as wrong as the last one!

That's not all there is to experiences of shame, or all that Lynd makes of them. Specifically my summary ignores the capacity of authority to assuage shame by sanctioning some actions that are normally condemned by the rules of society: "We were only following orders." It leaves out too the fear of shaming by a collective authority of one's peers for *not* breaking rules. That situation returns us to uncertainty, confronting us with a need to choose the map we adhere to. Exposure, isolation, and confusion can beset us from many sides. Some degree of "being shamed" may very well be incorporated in every self among us in various ways, including the way of strong, conscious denial. In any case, shame affects our feelings about our place in the world, about *entitlement*, about rights, about challenging rules instead of simply breaking them.

It is enough now, however, to observe the way that shame enters our lives as a means of teaching rules of behavior that enforce both manners and morals. The marks it leaves are never entirely obliterated and will direct the later responses we make to pressures and opportunities. Making a fool of oneself in public is hard to forget, and the recollection of it can lend strength to later injunctions to sit still, be quiet, and make the best of things as they are.

For parents, the question of shaming takes on a moral dimension that runs back at least as far as Rousseau's "Emile:" Is it right to shame one's children for doing what they don't know is wrong? There are alternate maps here too, and the one that deals with the pragmatic is usually the one that wins. Shaming works, and very probably with fewer painful results than noninterference would bring, overall. It certainly causes discomfort, but parents assure themselves that it's both kinder than punishment after the act, and safer than letting children run into danger. True, it would be better to forestall the mistakes that call forth this powerful sanction, but who can be sure of doing that? Well-intentioned teachers can't get into infant heads before the mistakes are made, they can only intervene near the end of the chain of events when improper behavior is well under way—when something nasty is halfway to the open mouth, when a screech announces that the child has been scratched or drenched or dirtied herself or been sick all over the kind lady who picked her up. No one knows what that child is going to do next until she starts.

Thus do parents and children muddle through the learning process together. Two kinds of fear get into parental responses: fear of real danger for their children whether social or physical, and fear of being shamed themselves. "What will people think if I let my child behave like that?" Both fears have sound pragmatic bases. Undisciplined children aren't pleasant to have around. They ought to learn manners early enough to make them reflexive because they are going to live, all their lives, in human communities with other people, and these people will expect that the rules in force will be more or less respected. Of course the rules may change, but some set of rules will always be there, and those who can't recognize their existence will run into unnecessary trouble. Moreover, parents who disregard rules about child raising will be judged harshly too, and their status will reflect on the children. On the whole it's better to know the rules, whether or not you decide in the end to break them. If you do, you'll be able to plan when and how to do it, and judge the consequences of your challenge rather than confusing the issue by accidental infractions.

Teaching rules is teaching a map for action, but let's step back from maps and their specifics once again, for more is being taught than the data and the given relationships. Learning rules also teaches us about connections in time: One thing leads to another. Events have consequences. Obviously, these connections can shift a bit too. Maps of etiquette and public morality are changeable and they are also affected by class and culture, and even more by gender. But the basic information, that events produce other events, is the very foundation of our ability to see patterns in the world around us: in people's behavior, the action of the stock market, the rise and fall of rock stars and politicians, as these things work themselves out on the four-dimensional maps of time and memory. Before any rules can apply and direct us toward proper behavior, we have to identify the situation we face and decide what set of rules is called for. The enormous market for books on how to behave, or succeed, or play a bridge hand, or impress your dinner guests with your table setting is evidence of our firm belief that what we do is not random.

If action isn't random, if one event leads to another, then knowing the right way to influence events can give a person the power to control the future; and that of course is exactly what the rules assure us they can do—teach us to direct and interact with the world around us. They limit what we're permitted to do, but that is done in order to make what we do *count*. Naturally children learn these directives eagerly as guides to action, just as they learn to recognize and to label nose and toes and the cat and Uncle Ben as recurrences, permanent bits of the world that place them in the world. Knowing the rules places us in the world of action and process and strengthens one's sense of self as a person who is aware of how and when to do this or that or the other thing adequately and gracefully, and of what not to do because it's inappropriate or dangerous and will have uncomfortable consequences. Or else, obviously, one learns that one isn't that sort of person because shame keeps breaking in.

We all know that girls learn different rules and roles from boys, and that proper behavior differs according to sex. Teaching gender distinctions is a major enterprise for the power to define. This is not just happenstance. The rules that govern gender behavior and affirm gender difference are primary in our lives; which does not mean that they can't be questioned. But they are integrated into the self very early, before the age of two, psychologists now believe, and they are present and active in every society that we know about.

For my purpose, the analysis of definition, these rules are also primary in a different mode. They are a test case of authoritative power and its techniques of operation. In gender images we're looking at phenomena where data are transformed into definitions. For the validity of gender difference is based on the fact of body difference: Men and women are physically different.

"What more do you want?" asks the power to define. "Just look at the variation in sex organs, musculature, beardedness, and so on and so forth. Isn't it indisputable that men are men and women are women?" And of course that's true, although we know that in some individuals the dichotomy is blurred. A few children are born with genetic anomalies in which the X or Y chromosome is doubled or absent, sometimes with physical consequences. Recently the medical profession has found it possible, also, to perform sex-change operations. "But," argues the power to define, "doesn't that just emphasize the difference? Who in the world would choose to go through a surgical metamorphosis if gender were a matter of easy choice? No one," it declares, "can argue with the facts drawn on the map of the body."

But that's not really the question, not in the world of social relations in which we live. What matters here isn't the data itself, it's the significance of what it's taken to establish. The *importance* of gender difference is held to be so great that it determines every other aspect of life. Anatomy is destiny, and if you're determined to change your destiny you have to be ready to alter your determining anatomy. This assumption of the all-important role of body difference also contributes to the companion assumption that homosexuality is deviant. "How can such feelings be normal," asks the power to define, "when they disagree with the evidence of the body?"

Well, here we can argue—not over the facts but over the assertion that these physical traits dictate one's place and one's conduct in life. If we accept that premise unquestioningly we are sliding from facts into preordained conclusions without taking thought. "Male and female created He them," says the Bible, and we take for granted therefore that Eve spins and Adam digs, and that all their endeavors in life will equally be limited and directed by the facts of bodily difference. We take it for granted in the face of our own certain knowledge that the kind of behavior and activity open to the two sexes has altered radically in our own time, and our amorphous realization that customs in this area always have been fluid around the world and throughout time. Bred to believing in timeless principles—and no doubt they exist, at least in terms of human time—we perceive them in situations where they are in fact masks for processes that can be changed, can be influenced by historical shifts and by personal strength and more often by a combination of both.

The power to define, in short, not only labels things, events, people, bits of data; it not only assigns them to differing maps of relationship drawn in terms of the underlying concerns of the community in which it operates, it also declares the relative importance of such events and of the relationships and the causalities that link them. Our subliminal awareness of our bodies, and the way that gesture, language, and appearance are used as a means for presentation of the self, this consciousness of physical personality, is open for use by the power to define; and one of the most forceful kinds of use is by shaming. Indeed, shame displays its own presence physically: We blush for our unworthiness.

Let us look at a prime example of how the power to define enforces the importance of gender difference by the use of shame. Once more we cast back to childhood and early learning. In our society and, as far as we know, in all societies, there are rules about dealing with bodily functions. With us, these functions are expected to be private and are also regarded as dirty. Most children run into shaming first during toilet training and learn, often painfully, that "exposure" in this part of life is particularly shameful. The stress of training has eased somewhat for American middle-class children during the last generation, but it certainly hasn't vanished. Like weaning, it's the occasion for a memorable confrontation between young child and adult, the demanding advent of discipline in an existence that had been pretty much ad lib until then. Both processes require children to adapt their physical selves to the rules of civilization as defined by the big people in charge and to observe laws they had no hand in making. Some children experience both adjustments, but all children are toilet-trained and in the process "the shame of being dirty" is a powerful argument for obedience.

What children give up in order to satisfy civilization's ideas about the importance of cleanliness is a point that doesn't have to be labored; psychoanalysts from Freud on have done that thoroughly. But, one way or another, dirtying oneself in public becomes a telling instance of shame. Indeed it crops up in other situations: Give it a twist one way and permission to do just this, à la Bohemian Grove conviviality, stands as a sign of comradeship. Give it a twist in a contrary direction, and shaming by defecation can be reversed, as when vandals dirty the premises they break into as an act of aggression and contempt. Symbolically it's a kind of rape of property by dirtying it, defiling it, leaving a mark of shame on it.

To sum up. Children learn to control their bodily functions early in life and pretty generally they run into some shaming as they do so. They live through a period (suffer through it) when what had been a normal necessary part of existence is redefined, colored by unpleasant emotions and classified as something to cover up; and that happens, obviously, to children of both sexes.

Then what about menstruation? What does the power to define have to say, and to direct as action, about a gender-related bodily function that can be labeled normal and necessary all you want but that can't be controlled by conscious will, and which produces an excretion that must be hidden? How is the female role and image, both internal and external, influenced? How is the acted-out behavior of women affected by a phenomenon that exposes us, but not men, to occasions for shame?

Please hold on to that question while another mightily relevant point receives our attention. In a patriarchal society (and what society isn't?) definitions are based on masculine experience because the definers—philosophers, sages, preachers, and professors—have been and still are male. Menstruation, by force of nature, is excluded from this experience; which experience, however, does include remembered lessons, deeply intimate and physical, often painful, about dealing with other bodily functions that were defined as dirty and stigmatized as shameful on similar grounds.

The process of definition, I have been saying, is one of

labeling data, of placing them in relationships, in patterns and on maps, of assigning importance both to data and to maps, and of prescribing the appropriate activities that follow from this identification. The function of definition—and it is vital for our understanding of the world—is to discriminate events and people and things from one another in order to identify them and thus to avoid confusion and occasions for shame. We invent rules to deal with frequent events and we establish causal connections, as distinct from simple coincidences. All of this makes definition a profoundly important mental exercise, necessary for keeping human beings straight in our links with each other and with the natural world.

But of course this whole essential activity has to be based on something out there, and the something, the data base, is what the definers have learned from life. Even Plato's eternal essences, if they existed, would have to make themselves known to human creatures somehow, by presenting themselves as knowable analogies to and through their earthly representations. No matter how firmly a priori axioms may declare that they are simple facets of ideal rational definitions of "the essential nature" of this or that, free from emotional perturbation and determined to avoid individual quirks, they still must ground their abstractions in the realities that have shaped the mentalities they speak to and through. Not only is the reality we experience the material that definitions process, it also supplies (as Hofstadter says) the basis for judgments made about this material by authority.

In judging and discriminating, that is, the definers turn to their own memory traces. What else could they use? They can enlarge the scope of material judged by polls and statistics, but anything they turn up still has to be processed by the minds of the judges, and what does turn up will be sorted through in search of what they consider relevant. What doesn't seem relevant will be discarded. The minds of the judges have been shaped by what's happened to them, personally and socially. It may be wide and curious knowledge, but nothing that hasn't touched them in some fashion can affect their judgments.

One more unspoken assumption: In drawing on their experience, the definers take it as *trustworthy*. They may feel that it isn't sufficient, and supplement it by further research, but they rely on the premise that what they know about life supplies sound ground for decisions. Their knowledge is *normal* knowledge, their reality *is* reality, their experience is paradigmatic and can be argued from.

What can that mean except that since men-the-definers don't menstruate, menstruation is felt as alien? At least for "normal human beings" who are designated by the generic pronoun "he"? True, in recent years doctors and psychologists have studied the phenomenon but not as part of their own lives; and that goes for most female researchers too, who are trained to work within the bounds of legitimate medical or psychological inquiry, which bounds are set by male definers. Few are the scientists who regularly proceed by confronting and analyzing their private experience and its effect on their outlook on the world. Freudian analysts, of course, must be analyzed themselves before they enter practice but analysis proceeds by a strongly systematized set of rules, with inbuilt values; masculine values.

For women, however, the physical phenomenon that's being defined as alien is not an abstraction at all, but our own experienced reality; the operation of our bodies, observed by someone else in the context of a whole society made up, in the realm of authority, by someone elses. We are expected to take the bodies we live with, our physical ground of being, as an inarguable sign of otherness and as a potential occasion for shame.

This singularity is felt, then, as an inescapable, always present condition that somehow enters into all female activities, a permanent mark of difference: "You Tarzan, me

Jane." It's not the only kind of human difference that takes on a permanent and ever-present quality—race and class also provide opportunities for being and feeling out of place as an inescapable part of one's identity—but gender is the oldest and most pervasive category of singularity. Both sexes, moreover, have lived for so long in a world that has been shaped by the importance of body difference that it's very hard to think ourselves away from it. It's rather like gravity, we're habituated to it. NASA spends some time teaching astronauts to adjust to zero-gravity but no authority has as yet tried to help humans adjust to states of zero-gender. So we go on habituating ourselves to behavior that automatically takes account of the maleness of men and the femaleness of women. For many people, indeed, the idea of change is frightening, in part because it is thought of as being reversal.

But well-adjusted men are perfectly capable of changing their behavior and directing their attention to other people in accordance with the situation that both are part of. What women want is the same kind of simple adjustability toward gender neutrality in conditions that call for it—conditions that are public rather than private, related to work and not to personal life. In fact, the increasing presence of women outside their old place at home is obviously forcing the invention of new kinds of intergender behavior in practice. Personal encounters of this kind work to dim the strength of old definitions; they are, in fact, a form of unconscious dehabituation, and as such they are valuable opportunities to make new roles acceptable.

But though the significance of bodily difference between the sexes may dim in certain circumstances, it is formidably present in maps for proper behavior. Morality, religion, politics, the economic world, literature and art, in all of these major realms of human affairs the effect of gender difference is built in and won't be altered, much less done away with, in a hurry. The symbolic value of physical characteristics is reinforced because they are easy to see, and indisputable as fact. "Different?" says the power to define. "Of course men and women are different. Just look at them!"

So as things stand now, the position and the perception of women are still deeply affected by appearance as it is understood and valued by masculine observations, which, needless to say, are almost equally valued by the great majority of women. On the other hand, doubts about old positions are based on female experience, what women do and feel and know as part of their changing lives. Neither of the two sorts of difference—the difference in experience from old female roles, and the physical difference between the sexes—is going to vanish, no matter how long the argument continues. What is really in question is, let me repeat, the importance of these differences to the conduct of ordinary life. They are important enough, however, to emphasize the two characteristics that are associated with bodily difference: women's otherness, and the physical inferiority that suggests that, like children, we need to be looked after.

Menstruation serves to justify both these labels. Whether otherness or inferiority comes first depends on the cultural maps and the mythologies of any particular society, but interpretations of the condition that serve this end have been documented around the world. If blood is seen in one culture as frightening, then the capacity of women to survive a monthly flow will be called eerie and linked to some magical force. These creatures are wounded but don't die. Normal human beings had better be wary of a capacity that suggests ties to witchcraft, and should avoid contamination by a fluid that is surely dangerous or polluting or both. Such beliefs have faded in our society but they are definitely part of our past. In Tudor England, historian Patricia Crawford notes, "an extreme work claimed that intercourse during menstruation would be fatal to the husband, so poisonous was the woman's monthly flow."[4] And the idea that menstruation has morbid influences still lingers; Crawford cites correspondence in the English medical journal, The Lancet, "on the subject of why flowers handled by a menstruating woman should wilt"[5] as recently as 1974, while an American friend recalls being cautioned by her mother against touching the houseplants while menstruating. These are visions of woman as "other."

If the definition of woman as inferior prevails, menstruation is likely to be seen as a kind of regular illness that makes it hard for females to undertake major enterprises requiring persistence and endurance. Once a month our ability to deal with events suffers. What would happen, a well-meaning male asked me recently, if a woman president were having her period at the moment when the Kremlin launched a nuclear attack? In a more dilute form such a fear acts as a deterrent to opening any sort of executive position to women. The definition stamps us as really belonging at home in privacy and concealment. This unfortunate ailment is a regrettable but unavoidable fact of life, one of those things that women have to put up with. Fortunately the female character is held to be fitted to endure such difficulties because we possess the feminine virtues of modesty and patience.

These differing views of menstruation may of course occur together. Let a distinguished anthropologist sum up the effect: Mary Douglas, considering the menstrual customs found in African and Australian cultures, remarks that "belief in the dangers of menstruation may be useful. . . . First, to assert male superiority and second, to assert separate male and female spheres."[6]

On the face of it, our ideas have changed. The extremes of avoidance techniques that in some societies imposed taboos and isolation on menstruating women don't affect us. But menstruation is still felt to be a potential disability, and it is still something to be concealed. I happened to be on the board of a writers' organization that processed grant applications when an early proposal for a study of menstruation came up for consideration. The embarrassment loose in the room was embarrassing in itself, as some of these intelligent professionals recoiled from the idea as disgusting and others tried to downplay it as a frivolous joke. Even today teachers of women's studies report that menstruation is the topic most difficult for their students to discuss in any analysis of gender roles, and whether or not it's still consciously regarded as something to be ashamed of, proper behavior requires that women *act* as if it were: Concealing its occurrence has to be planned and undertaken over and over and over. It's a normal, necessary bodily function and it is also something that must be hidden. Indeed the preferred way of dealing with the flow is by tampons, not napkins. We say that's more convenient, but what exactly do we mean by that word? One thing we mean is surely that tampons contain menstrual blood within the body, hidden more securely, unseen except by the person who must deal with it privately.

I don't want to belittle any kind of convenient, matter-of-fact, sensible ways to handle a minor physical nuisance. Indeed once we start granting importance to the convenience of menstruating women instead of thinking first about definitions based on male nonexperience, we're bringing our ideas down to actual earth. But even so we are still in tricky territory if we assume that *concealment* should be part of a definition of *convenience*. As long as hiding the condition is held to be of major importance, menstruation is treated as if it were shameful. Are tampons favored because they allow women to be active more readily than napkins do? That's certainly convenient. Or are they preferred because they hide the blood flow, and themselves, from observation? Which is the more important consideration? Both reasons are touched on in advertisements, but the second seems to be emphasized: No one will know you have the curse.

So now we come to the female label for the female phenomenon that has proved so useful in defining the image of women. What does it have to say about our picture of ourselves and our general condition?

Nothing simple. For women to call menstruation "the curse" implies that we see it as unpleasant and crippling, and that it carries the aspect of shame that Helen Lynd refers to as "irreversibility." It's part of our fundamental existence to live with a recurrent disability. In addition the name points to an outside and powerful cause. Things that invade one's private life and can also lay one open to public embarrassment happen to us for reasons that we've had no part in. Does that affirm that women are victims, powerless in the sense that we cannot change this condition? Does "the curse" imply that we deserve this fate, that otherness is related to inherent accessibility to evil? That in the person of Eve, perhaps, we made a terrible, shameful mistake and it turned out to be a sin? In any case, there's nothing we can do about it. And so, if we think in these semilogical, semisymbolic terms, irreversibility combines with exposure, isolation, and confusion, those hallmarks of shame.

Still, why in the name of goodness should we choose such an unattractive label? Pleasanter names have been used: Patricia Crawford cites "the flowers" or "the terms" as earlier English usages that don't emphasize the idea of blame for ancient wrongdoing.

No, our choice of label comes from somewhere else. At the deepest level it rises out of a strain of black humor. Patriarchal authority finds that hard to see: What's humorous about the facts of the female condition? But for those who partake of that condition, caustic jocularity can supply strength to bear what has to be borne, to ease acceptance of a gender role defined by an authority that takes pride in not sharing it, and to make resentment endurable while still declaring that its existence is just. Since time began we've been brought up to think that jokes at our expense are funny. That does encourage a joking approach to life, but one of a special kind. Female jokes are double-edged.

All humor springs from deeply ambiguous layers of lived experience. Ironic and double-edged, women's humor has also had to conceal its subversive thoughts behind a masking text: When we call menstruation "the curse," we are defining our social status. The name incorporates a bitter joke about our situation and illustrates the propensity of life for giving us opportunities to laugh because it hurts too much to cry. Who wants to confront the pain of reality when rebellion, we've been taught, is doomed to failure? So we make jokes that are definitions of the world as seen from below, mocking definitions that include the mockers and thus breach isolation. The message that the label "curse" carries, then, might run something like this: "Poor old Eve! She was curious and so she tried something new and—surprise!—it went wrong. So she ended by getting just what we all could have told her to expect, a curse from Himself up there. And it's still with us, friends. What a memory He's got!" Whatever the words of explanation, they are not commemorating sin or victimization or praising the righteousness of the Lord God who corrected our daring First Mother and left us His curse to remind us of her fault. No, we are mocking the familiar outrageous unfairness of the proceedings: "That's the Lord God for you, every time."

Responses like that make patriarchy uneasy. Can it be that we are laughing at shame even while we acknowledge its presence? Can it be that we don't take seriously our otherness, our eerieness, our childishness, that we dare to disagree with a judgment even while we bow to it? If that's so, the label we put on the unfortunate, unavoidable condition that females are lumbered with is neither modest nor abashed, it's a joke about masculine definitions! The kind of joke we're not supposed to make! Does this mean that somewhere underneath, in the depths of dangerous, duplicitous female secrecy, we harbor other subversive definitions of our own? Are we "others" perhaps conspiring to substitute them, one day, for the proper male maps of the world that have for so long explained events, defined the normal, and prescribed proper behavior?

Chapter 6

THE CORROSIVE RESENTMENT

expressed in bitter backstage humor, then, does not always lead to action, but instead may work as a substitute for action, a safety valve that lets private words take the place of public deeds. True, black humor is still valuable as communication: Your anger, your pain and frustration, are shared, it says. Other people are in the same boat; they live in the same conditions and speak the same language. Humor is an antidote to isolation. Decades before the rebirth of feminism in the 1960s, women were writing humorous best sellers that recorded a familiar litany of unhappy details of family life: Obsessed husbands dragged wives and children into ridiculous schemes for making money, or dreamed up unlikely programs for household management that backfired in terribly recognizable ways. Exaggerated they might be, but thousands of women read them and laughed; they knew this country and laughter was a relief.

But it didn't do much to alter anything; making pain more bearable doesn't promote plans to end pain. Changes in overall social attitudes grow out of external pressures. Of course these pressures make themselves felt as individual demands on individuals, but they are a product of shifting circumstances. In particular, women who had to earn incomes for themselves and for family support discovered that it could be done in new areas that had not been seen earlier as appropriate, had not been labeled For Women Only whatever this woman's class status might be. The jobs differed—a working-class girl could go into the mill or domestic service, a middle-class girl train as a teacher or librarian, but the limitations remained. It wasn't conscious resentment of confinement in the domestic sphere that launched a rebirth of women's liberation some twenty years ago. Instead an awareness of previous resentment came to consciousness as women learned that the whole setup wasn't really necessary, if it had ever been. They were capable of looking after themselves in a pinch, a lot more capable, at any rate, than they had realized. Contrary to some contemporary exercises in hindsight, no rosy utopias were imagined or promised, but the range of possible designs for living widened substantially.

Public changes certainly interacted with common attitudes. The kind of emotion that was expressed, and relieved, in black humor kept alive the skepticism about roles, which made the idea of alternative styles of life thinkable. Then, as the public world of economics and politics opened wider and action there seemed more plausible, attitudes began to shift. Experience was justifying the change. It brought old maps and their prescriptions for action into dispute because other sorts of action were going on. The directive to "grin and bear it" was less persuasive than it had been. Psychologically speaking, anger that had been suppressed could be turned outward and the energy that sustained it could be used in action.

Authority often seems to be worried about such a possibility before the agents of change themselves catch on. Even though black humor is full of self-mockery, it can become an irritant to the Establishment. An impartial observer could well wonder why authority is so sensitive to laughter that serves to hamper direct challenges from non-Establishment sources. One reason is surely that it illustrates the existence of a split in society, and therefore the chance that mainstream definitions are not being taken with total seriousness. In addition, the bitter jokes serve to identify events and occasions to be bitter about. Could they possibly foreshadow the invention of a new, contradictory map?

Moreover this humor-from-below is self-generating. It

offers its own definitions of value and no Establishment likes the idea of an underclass that can set up its own system of values. The jokes in question, if they are taken seriously, are pretty strong stuff. Suppose the victims stop laughing at what's unbearable? They have some caustic analyses of their position in the world and of the pressure points where change might take hold. For authority must surely suspect that it isn't simply ignorance or inferiority that keeps the governed majority sitting still; it's their own acceptance of a label that reads "inferior." Black humor may function for a while to strengthen this seeming resignation, but it can also become a seed of community strength and group commitment, factors that lie much closer to action.

As action for change begins, humor shifts its role. Now it supports and strengthens the effort for change. In the early days of desegregation, Greensboro, North Carolina, was the scene of sit-ins intended to open white-only eating places to blacks. Four students of the North Carolina Agricultural and Technical College staged the first, at a Woolworth store. Each came, as they later admitted, in spite of individual tremors because group loyalty outweighed personal fears. The protest grew, and on the following Saturday other students turned out, led by the NCATC football team. Young white students from the campus of the University of North Carolina branch at Greensboro also turned up, carrying Confederate flags, to protest the protest. "What do you want here?" they shouted at the blacks. "Who do you think you are?" The reference to Civil War history won a sharp response: "We're the Union Army," said the blacks.[1]

One joke doesn't make a summer, and Greensboro has witnessed ugly scenes since those days, but the impulse to laugh at Establishment labels keeps alive an awareness of other ways to describe "the way it has to be." Laughing at labels won't destroy them, but it can strengthen the courage and the comradeship that holds active protesters together and maintain a sense that alternatives exist.

Perhaps it's the Establishment that hears most clearly the underlying statement of possible substitutes for its prescriptions. An uncertain power structure, and few are entirely complacent, is likely to overreact. The governed are challenging not just the rules, which are secondary constructs and do shift from time to time, but also the premises on which the rules rest. That kind of deep challenge is an implicit claim on the power to define. It's impertinent, but more than that, it may even raise doubts in Establishment minds about its own maps and prescriptions. If they are losing their plausibility, is that just because they need to be presented differently? Or is it conceivable that they might really be false? Authority can get very nervous over that possibility, so nervous that repressing it comes to seem the only answer.

It isn't only the idea that is repressed in these circumstances. When definition by persuasion stops working, it's tempting to reach out toward force. Which has always been there to be used, needless to say, and has been used with full public acceptance, against criminals and traitors and troublesome deviants. If those who disagree with Establishment fundamentals can be relabeled as some of the above, they too can be disposed of forcefully. But this act of redefinition is best done plausibly—and visible force isn't compatible with plausibility. Authority much prefers to dispense with direct orders and, even more, with explicit police action to make those orders stick. The power to define works best, with least expensive fallout, when persuasion and propaganda do the job. For in fact and in politics, "nice guys" finish first, not last. They win by landslide approval, and what they win is a true prize, *legitimacy*. The rest of us agree that they know what they're doing, that the power they possess is theirs not just by force but by right.

Once the governed majority is convinced that our rulers are legitimately placed in that necessary position, we go along readily with the prescriptions for action that come from on high. Orders are orders, taken to be trustworthy, and policing their implementation isn't necessary. The community will faithfully police itself because it agrees with the official diagnosis of common problems and consents to follow the ordained rules for dealing with them. A government that operates through random force can certainly frighten the populace into acting *as if* it agreed with public proclamations on the propriety of mass arrests and detention without trial; but the very randomness of these interventions raises upsetting doubts. Does such an authority know what it's doing? Force cannot answer those doubts or allay growing distrust. It has no useful answer to resentment and bitter humor. It will never achieve what the persuasive power of legitimate government brings, a willing army of believers, eager to carry out the orders of the Establishment.

We will come back to force and violence as means for governance in later chapters; but there is a less obvious instrument for inducing proper behavior to be considered first: *public shaming.* We have seen that it works effectively to shape the behavior of individuals because it can enlist the self into disciplining itself. Public shaming—stigmatization—operates just as effectively as does private shaming. It invades the interior space of selfhood and calls up remembered experiences of childhood shame: of exposure, isolation, and confusion that seem unavoidable and without remedy. The purpose is the same too: control of public behavior.

Stigmatization uses a special kind of isolation in order to diminish the confidence and self-respect of those under attack. They are assigned to a group, but the group itself is labeled as worthless, alien, indecent, immoral, inferior, irreversibly ignorant—the pejorative adjectives that can be attached to these people are limitless. And to some extent, the label can be made to seem plausible. When people are grouped according to some element in their actual identities, and the whole body that shares the identity is given a degrading label, the self is given a reason for denying its own worth. "The race, the gender, the ethnic group into which you were born, the underclass of which you're a part, the sexual preference you manifest, these things mark you as lying outside the limits of social acceptability"—so says the power to define, as it takes an undeniable premise—one's gender, one's race—and sidesteps into an illogical conclusion.

This definition will be backed up by some kind of actual or threatened enforcement, sometimes legal and sometimes in the shape of social shunning. Economic sanctions are useful too. Lesbians and gay men know that some jobs are going to be closed to them if they live out their sexual preferences openly, that housing regulations can be used to disrupt their private lives, while threats of returning homosexual styles of life to illegality, always waiting in the wings, have now grown more immediate with the Supreme Court's 1986 decision upholding the Georgia law prohibiting sodomy. Black people have lived through a gamut of conditions of discrimination in work and housing and pay and simple access to public facilities. Shaming is not enforcement by physical means, but it represents the threat of enforcement if those who are stigmatized don't go along with "regular" social standards. Definition comes in again, ready to label any group whose customs may be different as being abnormal. If behavior is abnormal, it isn't entitled to protection from the community. This group has "chosen" to set itself apart.

There is evident here a slide in the function of definition itself: Propriety is being confused with normality, and normality with what is "natural." "Naturalness," as we've seen, likes to point to bodily difference as implying the existence of other kinds of difference. This sort of confusion gets into philosophy (where we will leave it, at least for the moment) and into daily existence. Directions for proper public behavior surround us like advertisements, telling us how to act, dress, present ourselves in gesture and speech, and whom to associate with if we want to be accepted as normal. "You don't want to get mixed up with those people," says the power to define. "They're oddballs." Such injunctions force individuals to demonstrate the naturalness of their ways of living and feeling and doing, or to be stigmatized as deviant, freakish, outlandish, monstrous, but in any case, outside the community in which they had thought they had a place. What can be less simple and natural than trying to act as if one were naturally, simply, something one isn't? When "naturalness" is confused with "propriety" we are being instructed to present not the self but the role.

That prescription creates an internal split in the psyche, a split that's deeply isolating because it confronts the self with doubt about its own identity and its own capacity for judgment. Doubts, of course, hinder independent action and shunt the doubter toward mere role-acting. Playing a role may become a mechanical skill that is cut off from internal emotional life. Eventually "behaving properly" moves so far from the reality of one's feelings that the person inside is insulated. Chekhov's disturbing story, "The Man in a Shell," illustrates perfectly this condition of living by public rules within an impermeable wall.

Psychic fission of this kind goes far deeper than the line drawn between etiquette in public and private enjoyment of one's freedom in one's leisure time. The threat of stigma doesn't just suggest toning down a public show of feelings; it's an order to deny one's feelings totally if they differ in any way from the standard required by one's role. For the stigmatized, private life does indeed become a closet, with a locked door. Even in a relatively tolerant age some degree of secrecy must surround a relationship that is likely to be labeled deviant. The need for concealment invites repeated tests of the value placed on the emotional bond. To a varying extent one is living against mainstream values. That kind of existence may be exhilarating just because it is daring, but maintaining a relationship that public opinion labels as dubious requires planning and arrangement. In itself, *managing* an affair diminishes its naturalness. One may counter social inconvenience by defiance, by asserting one's own counter-definition of normality, but though that's brave and healthy, it can't eliminate the public label. There's still a distance between "normal" and "stigmatized," even when the label is rejected. It's not only the label that needs changing but also the map markings from which it derives.

Blackmail trades on such a situation and so does pornography. If the road to pleasure requires violating rules, violating rules may take on the quality of pleasure in itself. Again, if violation grows too dangerous, fantasy will substitute itself for activity and fantasy invites its dreamers to retreat from activity into passive fancy. The link between wanting and imagining some desired goal and going to work to get it is broken, and with it goes the integration of the self into a person who can be both private and public without shifting one's nature.

As we've seen, the retreat offered to children from unhappy experiences of shame is for them to acknowledge their mistakes and be forgiven because they didn't know any better. We've seen too that in adult societies the acceptance of a pretended status of childish inferiority is regularly offered to rule breakers as the way to excuse themselves for blunders. But choosing to retreat amounts to a rejection of autonomous power, and that's what authority wants. Learn better, it says. In time you will know how to follow the rules (our rules) naturally (which is a contradiction in terms). Until you do, be obedient and do as you're told.

But how can anyone "learn" to rid oneself of one's past, or to change one's sexuality, to alter gender or color or ancestry? Wiping out the past is a denial of the reality that shaped this individual and supplied the experience on which she or he must depend for any decisions or choices. Because we have nothing left on which to base independent judgment, we become open to official propaganda and ready to accept the opinions of any passing expert. Like patriarchy, chosen naïveté returns us to childhood. With one important difference: Children do need to learn, and shame is used most often as a temporary tactic.

Stigmatizing adults is something else. It isn't meant to be temporary but to establish a permanent status of disability, and to enforce it by crippling the self. Substitute passivity for ambitious, directed action. Make retreat and cowardice habitual. "Explain" that such behavior is right because "these people," alas, are inferior in one way or another and can't be independent. Authority can thus short-circuit dissent before it begins. Indeed, it can go on to use the absence of dissent as proving that the governed who don't revolt in the face of provocation are indeed inferior. Wouldn't they rebel if they were capable of doing so? So the acceptance of stigma can become a stigma in itself.

The power of shame as a social control has another source as well. If we look again at our contemporary codification of definitions, the dictionary, we find that the root of "stigma" is precisely the creation, by design, of a permanent bodily difference: a *brand*. Classically that is a deliberate burn-scar, but the cropped ears of a thief have served just as well, and so did the numbers tattooed on the skins of prisoners in Hitler's camps.

Body difference is being invented where it didn't exist. An inferior, a deviant, is being labeled in a fashion that is visible. And since definitions (says the dictionary) designate the essential nature of this thing or person or process, the presence of an interior "essential nature" is made public by a permanent mark. Here we see once more the power attributed to permanent physical difference as evidence of the validity of definitions. What our own eyes tell us seems convincingly plausible.

In the case of stigmatization, the idea of a permanent status has a particular use. All definitions aspire to permanence and though few of them achieve it *in toto* and forever, the ones that label human beings do often manage to mingle themselves with something that *feels* permanent. Like visible evidence for other people, the interior sense of the self, the person who lives in this body, is a very convincing witness to reality. If the person labeled has to agree that the label is accurate in any way—that one is indeed female, black, Jewish, lesbian, and so on in a world that regards these qualities with distaste—the two permanences can slide toward each other and combine. If the shoe fits, the old proverb condemns us to wear it. If the label has any basis in fact, we have to fight like the devil to keep reality clear and distinct from the invidious value that the label has been assigned. If that is impossible, the self itself becomes the carrier of stigma.

In spite of the dictionary and the aspirations of definitions toward permanence, values and reputations do actually change with time. But stigma seems to be harder to get rid of than a sense of worth. Habituation plays a hand here. Waking in the morning, every morning, the carrier of stigma is faced with another day of behaving in a mode that violates the person inside. Self-discipline becomes self-abuse. In a double role, one part is always fantasy. Who can be sure which is which? Perhaps the fantasy lies in refusing to accept the public label.

In our time, that kind of experience, we like to think, is less common than it once was. Aren't we democratic, don't we believe in equality? In fact, an unwelcome label awaits all of us who live long enough: We grow old. Which is not to cry down a general chance at longevity but just to point out that aging is a process that includes lessons in role changing and in altered perceptions. Especially for women, whose status has always depended on the appearance that is presented to the public, the dwindling of attractiveness very clearly means lessened importance. One has to approach people in a different style, and there's no charm school to turn to for instruction. Do we get humble? Do we get bitchy? Do we draw back from contacts?

And how about the person inside? How much of this change is real? one has to ask oneself. How much is simply part of other people's vision, distorted by their own dislike of messengers from unwelcome future times? Here is bodily difference in action. "Staying young" becomes almost a social duty, but of course one can never really run fast enough to stay in the same place. And then to the shame of aging is added the stigma of pretense to an age one isn't. Here comes another double bind. Not to try to look and seem younger is wrong, but so is trying too hard. Perhaps the popularity of retirement communities is partly based on the fact that living with one's contemporaries means that one stays visible and individual as an unlabeled person longer than one does in the world in general.

So public shaming of a group is a different sort of social control from the shaming used to teach children the rules they need to know. Offering adults the label of child isn't a temporary return to a stage of life we can count on growing through. The smiling side of patriarchal authority, holding out the carrot of care as opposed to the stick of blame, never tells us that care goes with dependence, and that independence is not going to arrive with the passage of time and the proper learning of lessons. In childhood, we looked forward to an inevitable change of status with the advent of maturity. Not now. If, as adults, we try to move out of the novice role, the label of "child" with its promise of care will shift to nastier names: rebel, outcast, fool, or crazy.

Those labels are justification for using force, whether economic, symbolic, or actual. Stigmatization minimizes such use by holding it back, as a threat. For when the governed accept the label of dependent and inferior, they are still granting to authority the right to define the world and prescribe what ought to be done there: in fact, to rule. Minimizing the use of force makes ruling less costly. It's expensive to police a rebellious populace with a mind of its own. In troubled times it can be so expensive that distracted Establishments find the idea of dictatorship alluring because it seems to promise an end to arguments over means and ends and to ensure that people will do as they're told.

That's illusion. Aside from the sheer monetary cost of police and secret agents and counterspies and infiltrators, of prison buildings and guards and security, dictatorships are expensive because they have to sacrifice process to structure. They lose flexibility. They cannot respond easily to change in the world by adapting themselves to new needs. Dictatorships offer up inventiveness to the idol of permanence on an altar labeled Status Quo. Even before the populace consciously distrusts the Establishment, the Establishment has begun to distrust its citizens and to discount their experience. Slowly the governed become invisible and above them the vital cadres of the implementers, who must see that policies are carried out, are told to be dumb, to follow orders without asking questions. But these are the very people who are charged with making orders work, and if they can't report on orders that don't work, top-level decisions are necessarily made in the dark. Machinery is set in motion, and the mechanics who know how it works are forbidden to touch it. When it breaks down, it's not inefficiency that is blamed, but treason. The intimate knowledge of needs and limitations that makes smooth operation possible is outlawed. Forced labor, following rules unrelated to the end product, is always expensive labor. Hitler and Stalin both worked prisoners to death, and the installations put in place were noted for a high rate of failure.

Moreover, everything that is planned and done must be thought up and programmed by the Establishment, for no one else can be trusted. A small group of people is labeled "experts" and charged with making decisions. But the longer they stay in office, the less will they know about what has happened in their fields since they became administrators and the less will they be able to discriminate, through Hofstadter's "common sense," between useful new ideas and fantasies. Standards become static, and if the Company Way can't be criticized, it will never know the magnitude or the consequences of its errors. Dictatorships aren't a cure for disruption, they're a product of it, a symptom instead of a remedy.

Our own supposedly democratic history offers a clear example of economic dictatorship, spelled out and accepted originally as legitimate, in the institution of slavery. As its legitimacy began to be questioned, a need to justify it morally produced a myth in which black people were described as children, dependent and needing the care that capable white masters provided. Of course that wasn't the only myth applied to blacks; they were also primitive, animal, and if human, members of an innately inferior race. Black "black humor," preferring the power of animality to childish dependence, proceeded to make the word "bad" a synonym for autonomous, self-directed action and judgment. For the white masters, however, the label of dependent child was best. It avoided the cost of regarding all blacks as forever dangerous, which would have demanded continuing measures of protection and distancing in space. As we can see today in South Africa.

But in fact, as Eugene Genovese notes in his discussion of "The World the Slaves Made," *Roll Jordan, Roll,* blacks and whites in the antebellum South lived pretty close together, mainly on small farms or middling-sized plantations. Huge factory farms, with distant slave quarters, were rare in the United States, though typical of the West Indies. An occasional rumor of incipient slave revolt kept the idea of black danger alive, but precautions taken then were improvised and were quickly forgotten. My own grandfather remembered one such rumored threat (as he wrote in a memoir for his children) when, at the age of nine, he had nursed a horse pistol "nearly as big as myself" through one long Georgia night. (He survived to become a passionate enemy of slavery who faulted Lincoln for his delay in proclaiming Emancipation.) But that nightwatch had taken place in a town; on the farms, however, a factual, if unequal, intimacy with their slaves was forced on the masters by circumstances. Fearing them was neither practical nor dignified.

In addition, the presence of slaves raised a problem of political ethics. How was slavery to be justified? Patriarchy, paternalism, offered a mode in which "the peculiar institution" could be legitimized. That problem had not bothered earlier ages, but morally, this elite of slave owners was descended from the founders of a new nation claiming to be a land of the free. And they were mainly upright, churchgoing Christians whose religion spoke of the brotherhood of man under the fatherhood of God. The patriarchal view of blacks as dependent children "grew out of the necessity to discipline and morally justify a system of exploitation,"[2] writes Genovese. Note the idea of *discipline* here; not discipline of blacks—that of course is assumed—but of whites, in order to limit exploitation. For pragmatic reality had to take account of the end of the African slave trade. Now the existing labor force could no longer be replenished by legal imports. Now slaves had to be kept in conditions good enough to encourage them to reproduce themselves and supply new generations of labor. There was also the capital investment in the work force; Hitler and Stalin could sweep up new drafts for the camps and the gulags at will, but these people had money value. They had been bought and they could be sold.

Add to this underground awareness of economic requirements the simple facts of living in fairly close quarters. It made inevitable some sense of blacks as individual people, not mere ranks of alien others. If care of these folks was necessary in money terms, and if daily shared experience made them known (though less, of course, than the whites were known to the blacks), then the relationship fitted the label paternalism. Morally it assured the slave owners that they were acting for the good of their dependent slave children, the "darkies" whom they understood so much better than any reforming northerner could. They disciplined them as did good fathers, not sparing the rod. They indulged their fancies by permitting celebrations, gatherings, and storytellings; they listened to the songs and spirituals through which the slaves were both assimilating and evaluating white culture while preserving what they could of an African identity, and found them amusing. It was as close to justification of bondage as a morally anxious slaveholding society could come.

It's not surprising that the masters took the doctrine of paternalism a good deal more seriously than did the slaves. So firmly did the whites credit their own goodwill that they assumed the blacks must be grateful to them and they tended to be indignant if gratitude was not forthcoming. A Virginia planter wrote in angry puzzlement, after Emancipation, "I begin to believe that they are without gratitude. Mine appear to have forgotten all the kindness and lenity with which they have been treated by me and my family."[3] Remarkable as such self-deception seems today, "the masters desperately needed the gratitude of their slaves in order to define themselves as moral beings,"[4] writes Genovese (noting the human need for legitimization of oneself by accepted definitions.) The label of "father" was mythic, but it served its purpose.

Or so the planters thought. The slaves, needless to say, assessed the relationship differently. If they were dependent, did they not work off any debt for the care they were given by their own labor? When the masters declared that they had a "duty" to provide for them, did not the very word "duty" wipe out any obligation on the part of the slaves, by admitting that these dependents had a right to provision and care? What they had agreed to deliver, perforce, was not gratitude or childish affection, it was physical labor. "Out of necessity they had made an uneven agreement, but it was nonetheless an agreement,"[5] Genovese sums it up: an inequitable social contract, but still a contract. They were not children, but workers. Authority greeted this exercise in redefinition as ingratitude merging into betrayal, thoroughly improper behavior.

There's a lesson in the logic of definition here. Definitions lump things together, things that can be considered similar: Slaves and children are similar because both classes are dependent on others who are self-actuating adults. Now, lumping together of people and entities and processes is necessary. Nothing in life is exactly the same, so that labels do have to stretch in order to pull things that are alike under the roof of one word. Then we can recognize these similar sorts of things when we run into them again.

But similar isn't the same, matching isn't identity. A useful match must be able to stand up to the same rule of plausibility that makes any definition acceptable. When the parent-child relationship is tugged into a place where it passes as representing the link between masters and slaves, the bounds of acceptability are being breached. In the service of authority, the power to define can be used to set up seeming likenesses, and in this confusing world we are often willing to accept them because they bring order into disorder. Science and philosophy, religion and magic, and always politics have been trying to establish linkages among the events of our world forever and a day. These connections are laid out for us, accepted by us, and then, often, they fade. Left-handedness, for example, is losing its importance very quickly in our society but a generation or two ago children were apt to be trained and scolded out of it. In many other cultures too there existed, or still does, an association between the left hand and bad luck, with inferior status including femaleness, with the profane as opposed to the sacred—quite simply, with the "sinister."[6] Where it is now a natural quirk to us, it's still deviant, still appropriately sinister, in other places.

Such fading of definitions as they decline into superstitions and finally vanish is, perhaps, a shadow equivalent of improper behavior itself: the passive voice, so to speak. Both are unconscious and unplanned, simply a response to an awkward reality that seems to vary unexpectedly from old descriptions. In one case, a directive—Use your right hand!—is already losing its importance, so that failing to follow this order doesn't matter much. In other cases, prescriptions hang on stubbornly demanding obedience even though obeying gets harder and harder until finally these outworn directives fall into limbo. If only the first response could always happen! Then we wouldn't have to break rules because they would change by themselves.

But only idiot optimism is going to assume that false definitions will inevitably disappear without being disproved, and then disproved again. Between human perception and what a current society needs to run smoothly lie the maps and the priorities and the prescriptions, and any or all can get out-of-date, but persist. Any hope for success has to lie in the record of human survival and adaptation. Somehow, so far, judgment and common sense have been capable in time of distinguishing—not truth, that is far too abstract to be proved—but pragmatic plausibility, what's likely to work. Discrimination of that sort can show us when and where apparent similarities are growing irrelevant and unimportant. We know very well today that human beings owned as slaves are not "similar" to children and that the southern masters were profoundly and sincerely wrong.

On the other hand, has the definition of black people as dangerous creatures who had better be kept at a distance from white respectability and especially from real power fallen out of our minds? We had better look at the way in which the power to define upholds authority by distancing the governed from their rulers as being alien, abnormal, and incapable not by weakness but by difference.

Chapter 7

DEFINITIONS THAT FOCUS ON OTHERNESS

separate the group that is so labeled from power more
harshly and more irrevocably than do those that simply
speak of ignorance or immaturity. Treating adults like children certainly diminishes their status, their entitlements,
and their autonomy, but it still offers some small, mean ac-
knowledgment of their presence. It also holds out a half-
hearted promise that one day they might grow up to be
mature adults who can win approval from the powerful pa-
triarchs who manage the world. That goal appeals to the
hopes and ambitions of the less powerful even as it ties these
hopes to the advantages offered by the Establishment.

But when people who have been given a status as children begin, instead, to be treated as alien, the chances of advancement that were offered them earlier are withdrawn.
Now they are being labeled as different, so different that
they can never expect to learn proper grown-up ways of
doing and seeing and feeling. The qualities that define their
"essential nature" are held to be less and less human, less
normally civilized. True, an Establishment often sees both
immaturity and difference when it looks at an out-group,
and it will emphasize whichever condition seems more pertinent to its own purposes at the time. Some of the governed
may be described as possible learners if there is work that the
ruling clique needs done. Such people will require control
and direction in doing these chores, but they will be taken
care of in return. Imperial governments from Rome to Brit-
ain have been happy to use ambitious "natives" as function-

aries in the bureaucracy, or as auxiliary troops. Immigrants have been allowed to operate in areas where older inhabitants prefer not to work or have even been imported for these purposes, as were the Chinese who built the western stretches of America's railroads.

Within a society, too, groups that have not traditionally been permitted to perform some kinds of labor can move into new careers, but they still come with an aura of difference. Role behavior has to change as new occupations are taken up and the old left behind, and the process may involve both the role changers and those who interact with them in awkward situations. As we all know, ambitious young women have for some years now been flooding into the professions and into the lower-upper reaches of management, but the pioneering stage is by no means over. Rules for proper behavior are ambiguous and subject to change. At times one should "act like a woman," while at other times, a capacity to "act like a man" is clearly demanded. As yet no proper label indicates which prescription to follow; indeed, it's still uncertain whether these incomers are novices who can be taught the rules, or whether they are basically "other." We aren't rid of doubts and queries about "the essential nature of woman" by a long shot. As things stand both labels can be called on according to the needs of relevant authority and its own degree of anxiety.

A historical parallel suggests the difficulties in relabeling and redefining that go with a public change of status: the fate of blacks in the South and in the Caribbean after Emancipation. The masters who were stunned at the "ingratitude" of the newly freed were more common in the States, where some degree of intimacy had been widespread, but everywhere the image of black people shifted strongly toward "otherness." Any care they had been given was withdrawn at once. The ex-slaves were now free to look after themselves, and if they found it hard, it was their own fault. Where great plantations abounded, as they did in the sugar islands, there was a formal effort to re-create the conditions of forced labor by other means: by the importation of contract labor from Asia, by brutal physical punishment, by taxation, and by severe restrictions on the ownership of land by blacks.[1] In the States, after the end of Reconstruction, less formal economic methods, combined with Jim Crow laws, created a de facto bondage through sharecropping. A family, working rented land and buying through controlled outlets, could never quite manage to pay off the loans it had to make for seed and equipment and necessities.

Meanwhile as black dependence lessened, social distance grew. The slaves, who had been labeled "childish" in the past, retained the traits of immaturity that went with the name: In the eyes of whites they were still irresponsible, lazy, and unwilling to work. But the adjectives that marked them as "other" grew in importance: They were primitive, they were animal. A threat to civilization was thought to be foreshadowed by revolution in Haiti and rebellion in Jamaica.[2] If the white South was less apocalyptic in its attitude, the reaction was no doubt due to the facts of population. In the islands the blacks were a huge majority. Just the same, public shaming, the insistence on demonstrated inferiority by everyday, habituating segregation, combined with threats of force and force itself to establish the idea of apartheid as a basic social prescription in the States as well as in the islands to the south. Plenty of white southerners claimed that the old system was more humanistic than the new; and it's arguable, in theory, that one can feel closer to a "child" than to "a dangerous animal." But of course, the argument is based on the idea that only these two labels were appropriate: "Equality" was out of the question. Black freedom, in the minds of post–Civil War whites, could only go with a place outside the community, for the place the blacks had held as slaves was tied to their acceptance of dependence.

In a muted form, the psychological demands of role changing still affect the image of women today. Many black people find analogies between their social status and that of women displeasing: White women haven't been held as slaves, and their household labor wasn't and isn't forced in the way that black labor was. And that's certainly true. But if we can think of the analogy as existing *in the minds* of the White Male Establishment, I think we can see a clear similarity. Blacks and women are seen as hovering between identities of "children" and "other." Both have been distanced from independent uses of power, though the distancing has been achieved in different ways. Even the idealized purity sometimes ascribed to women suggests that they should not mix with power politics, lest they be corrupted. When we look at the power to define, and not at its objects, I think we do see the same tools at work. They are the natural, timeless instruments of definition and prescription. Role changing, that is, isn't easy for anyone. Admission to areas of society that have been forbidden in the past can be like admission to the fun house in an amusement park, where those entering find themselves falling through trapdoors, walking into blind alleys and seeing themselves mocked by reflections in distorting mirrors.

Moving out of an old role, in addition, requires more than simply learning existing roles in the new area one enters. The old role had its own values. Should they be thrown away? True, the new role may declare itself superior to the old, but is that really true, true throughout? If so, why are these superior folk letting inferiors in? Even if you, as an ambitious incomer are happy to enter and willing to take your chances, sure that new is better, what do you face and what do you do when the remnants of past behavior, or the marks of bodily difference, set you off as unlike the clever people who have always lived in this part of the world and learned the ropes young? For immigrants almost always carry a scent of strangeness, and strangers are to be feared in any comfortable social space.

It's no use to claim that you, the incomer, are a harmless, childish learner, eager to grow into maturity. As an incomer, you cannot control the definitions that label you. Strangers are, per se, strange. The original settlers can't tell what they might do, nor can they be sure how to cope, themselves, with those chancy intruders. How can the old inhabitants trust them if their languages and gestures can't be comprehended? Keep them separate then, in order to keep safe; so say those who feel themselves invaded. Then barriers go up in the conviction that they can't be penetrated by goodwill. Now there can only be bad will. Laws to prevent violence from "them" may justify violence against them.

The ability of black people to endure and survive the measures of human wrong put in place to control them is a testament to one aspect of human nature: It contains the essential qualities of courage, stamina, and imaginative daring, all hailed as virtues by white cultural Establishments, whether or not their members do themselves exemplify such qualities. But the recent growth among whites (not all, of course) of a capacity to perceive the full and equal humanity of black people is also due to historical circumstances. In the last couple of centuries, processes of social change have speeded up. In so doing, they have shaken the solidity of ancient definitions. The label of "savage" applied to an underclass has not always dimmed so quickly. Our own Western civilization grew out of a society in which a servile stratum had been described as "animal" for a thousand years.

"The early medieval peasant," writes Jacques Le Goff, "is [seen as] a barely human monster and subsequent literary production was to continue to present him in this guise. . . . Peasants were great, ugly huge-headed beasts with wide eyes fixed in an animal stare."[3] In addition, these half-human creatures were described in the writings of the time as "vicious by birth and nature, lechers and drunkards," whose sins were made manifest by their physical defects: that is, *by body difference*, that familiar basis for labels, which set them apart from the better-fed masters of the land they tilled. If poor food and filthy conditions of life produced blemished skin, they were labeled as "lepers" and exiled to the road and the wild. Rustic superstitions declared that they were pagan at heart and thus alien to the sacred community as well as to the secular world. If religion touched them in any way, the legends testify, it was as the occasion for virtue in others. If they called forth the charity of the saints, it was to demonstrate that those who helped them *were* saints. Only rarely could they value what was done for them and they were much inclined to fall away from the teachings of the Church into loutish heresies, demon worship, witchcraft. Above all, they were dangerous.

Such characterization did not just permit the exploitation of these "medieval Calibans," it encouraged it. As late as 1737, in the great century of European Enlightenment, a Bavarian official described a typical peasant as "a hybrid between animal and human." These creatures were regarded as unteachable as well, or nearly so, and as "thoroughly lazy, mendacious, people who are accustomed to do the little work that they do only under invective or blows,"[4] an opinion that was repeated over and over by the masters of slaves in America. Black or white, white or black, most of us alive in America today are descended from one or another sort of "bestial monster."

But separating classes and sects and races and genders from one another does not stop at polarizing the social world and dividing it by two into "us" and "them." It leads to a more complex operation: the invention and establishment of a hierarchy. Dividing the world in two is only a first step: "they" are divided again and again. As George Orwell remarked in his political satire *Animal Farm*, some are more equal than others. The less equal remainder are split into multiple subgroups that are separated not only from authority but also among themselves.

It isn't only variety that is being laid out here, though these groups may in fact be made up of people who command different crafts or trades. Variety becomes vertical, and it isn't so much the skill that one possesses that counts, it's the rank allowed to its possessor. The advantage to authority is easy to see. Once a system of grades has been set up, the great people at the top don't have to enforce the separations between one rung on the ladder and the next: Occupants of a higher rung will fight to keep those below from climbing. They will see such ambitious aspirants as enemies, not as potential allies.

Rank, however, isn't all that is present. For those on the ladder, *the hierarchy becomes a community*. It provides a sense of belonging to a social entity, and thus grants a basic identity: not exactly who one is, but what one is as a member of a known world. Hierarchy is also seen as necessary structure, lending coherence to what might else be a formless and casual grouping. Levels of aristocracy, a "chain of command" in an army, come to seem the obligatory way for getting things done in the real world. True, the structure that is created this way is biased, but inequality is taken to be worth a safe niche within a known group by the unequal themselves.

Creating a hierarchy, in fact, is equivalent to assigning priorities. The map of society now supports human beings whose importance varies. In some times and places, individual capacity can make a structure more flexible, but any social structure tends toward permanence, and ranking becomes built-in, learned and practiced, recognized and accepted. When belonging becomes a higher good and patriotism overrides individual ambition, the poor put up with poverty and the oppressed with oppression, and live vicariously through the glory of the glorious beings at the top. Rank and difference imply each other. Conversely, equality is confused with sameness.

Of course the people at the bottom of the ladder are not totally accepting. They would like to do better. But usually they would like to do *just a little* better, the amount of "better" that they can easily imagine as possible. Too much "better" often seems threatening: It can expose you to committing terrible blunders and running into shaming for being out of place. Minimal ambition, however, promotes hostility: One is ready to fight the people on the next rung up, while those on the next rung see this ambition as a threat. The ancient, ubiquitous technique of "divide and rule" keeps the Establishment established by directing disagreement among the governed into feuding among the governed. Internal hostility preserves the status quo.

Needless to say, the value of hierarchical ranking is not usually presented to the world as simply beneficial to the people at the top. Instead the need for graded societies is held to be validated by their likeness to the order of the natural world. There each bird and beast, each plant or tree, has its place in a great chain of being. Isn't the division of the human world then symbolic of this natural order? Isn't physical reality clearly made up of different sorts of creatures filling different ecological niches, appropriate each to each, with our human selves at the peak? It's easy to overlook the fact that different species of animals are truly separate from one another because evolution has made breeding among them infertile if it is possible at all. We look at the message of the metaphor and not at scientific data and analogize social rank to what we see out there in the physical world. Is not this arrangement a divine creation of the Lord God, or at least a necessary, natural way things ought to be? Is it not, therefore, an ideal that human society should copy?

Agree to that proposition and any attempt to disprove the relevance of this familiar metaphor becomes highly improper. The idea that law and order are tied up with status seems to have been endemic throughout history. It resembles the appeal to body differences as a basis for gender roles and the racial and class distinctions that mimic them. Definitions are inventive in finding ways to establish their plausibility by pointing at what is right there before us: the horizon line that proves the earth is flat, the undeniable-by-our-eyes movement of the sun around the earth. In the same way, human beings have been sure that blacks differ deeply and essentially from whites, peasants from masters, men from women. How childish, how silly (or else how wrong-headed) to argue with such evidence!

Historically, then, social distance tends to harden into ranking, which then becomes permanent as hierarchy. Of course the sequence is affected by economic, social, and cultural change: In a comfortable and complacent society like our own, the sharply defined traditional ranking familiar in the past is not obviously present. Indeed this highly mobile nation dislikes admitting that rank exists at all. Americans like to tell pollsters that they consider themselves middle-class, while television offers a common body of culture available to all.

But even so we tend to act as if some kind of rank existed. Fame, and to a lesser degree, wealth; "making it" in a public way, in politics or entertainment (and the two grow closer every day); business success that is mythicized by publicity to produce heroes, like Lee Iacocca or John DeLorean—these are areas where degrees of importance are clearly marked. The English, it used to be said, "dearly love a lord." Contemporary America loves tycoons and stars from the entertainment world. Equally it fears an underclass and seems as ready to use violence against these threatening, violent creatures as ever did those ancestors of ours who found it necessary to defend themselves against freed slaves or rebellious serfs. Those who like theoretical speculation might consider whether the weakening of traditional hierarchical ranking has also weakened a sense of permanent, stable community. Conservatives would say yes, I presume: Social mobility is dangerous, it threatens the orderly structure of the world. No doubt it does. And no doubt that is why the power to define is eternally ready to rebuild some sort of ordered ranking so that "the rich man in his castle, the poor man at his gate" will know where they belong and how they are to behave properly. Nonetheless, as Galileo said, the world does move. Reality does shift. And society must somehow adjust.

That kind of adjustment means that old maps must be redrawn or new ones invented. New or not, however, the techniques for inventing them do not change, though the actual means are of course updated. Shaky analogies drawn from observation of the physical world seem to confirm the inevitability of social status, as if rank were akin to difference among species. Indeed the idea of rank invades the animal world to designate the lion as "king of the beasts." Within the human species, any distinguishable physical traits have long been taken to separate one group from another, going on to assign such a group to a place in the current hierarchy. The most easily seen differences imply the strongest separation. Color as a sign of rank not only distinguishes black from white, but influences status within the black community itself, where a light skin has often been defined as preferable. The self is thus enlisted against its own physicality. Another technique for separation among minorities showed up recently in troubled South Africa, where those labeled "colored," people of mixed race, were granted a semblance of power by being permitted to elect representatives to an assembly that, itself, could do little but meet, talk, and approve government policy. Things have been moving so fast in South Africa that the attempt to formalize rank among minorities seems to have had little effect, but the intention is instructive. Not only were the coloreds invited to separate from the blacks, but the blacks were invited to resent any coloreds who approved the government's action.

Not only is body difference itself important as a means of assigning rank; the presentation of the self by language, gesture, and dress contributes. In Shaw's *Pygmalion* we witness Eliza's ability to pass from lower to upper class as she absorbs the lessons of Professor Higgins. No matter that class difference isn't shown only by speech; Eliza's style of dress also changes, but Shaw makes his point with force. Regional accents also affect ideas about identity and can even indicate status. At times, top people have chosen to use a language completely different from their inferiors'. In the seventeenth and eighteenth centuries more and more upper folk used nonnative languages: Czech nobles spoke German, educated Finns spoke Swedish, and in Russia the nobility went on speaking French as long as there was a nobility. When I was studying Russian, my teacher was amused to find that conversations in the copy of *War and Peace* that we were using had been largely translated *into Russian* by Soviet publishers from the French she recalled in the old family copy she had read as a child.

Marking by language is most useful in small groups where strangers come close enough to be heard. Costume, being visible, is seen at a greater distance. Our own society may seem to blur class distinctions in dress, but they are still there. We prefer to think of clothes as being simply a matter of personal taste, with some necessary attention to changes of fashion, though we don't want to look "inappropriate." But inappropriate in what way? To our own particular selves, or to the "what" rather than the "who" we happen to be? Both elements are present, while the fact that we have such choices at all depends on cash income. Clothes are so inexpensive now compared to the slowly assembled, carefully preserved costumes of our ancestors that wearing old garments often takes on a new meaning. Old money likes old clothes, and Cold Roast Boston will appear at times in the ancient tweeds of its fathers.

Even so, being appropriate may demand more than we want to spend. Why else does the New York Yellow Pages give more than four pages to listing "Formal Wear—Rental and Sales"? Going to a ball or a wedding makes proper behavior in dress a prerequisite for attending. Cinderella only met the prince through the kind intervention of a fairy godmother, whose first act was to transform her costume from rags to knock-'em-dead elegance. Without the proper clothes she would never have got in. Having once been mistaken for a waitress myself, I know now that one shouldn't wear a black dress with a white collar to a large reception.

In our day such minor confusions aren't very upsetting,

but they point to a special meaning that clothes can convey: status defined by uniform. "Clothing," said Erasmus, "is in a sense the body of the body," and when the meaning of costume is defined as clearly as it is by uniform, we are looking exactly at a mimicry of bodily difference.[5] Uniforms state that the wearer belongs to a special group, and often to a rank within it. If there's any element of choice present, it's in the decision to join that group: Every member of the armed services in the United States today has made such a choice, though some may have done so as a way of escaping from individual stresses in favor of life as the anonymous player of a role; not a "who" but a "what." But let a military draft be reinstated and individual decision turns into random selection; those who are drafted are expected to serve and are prosecuted if they refuse without an acceptable excuse. During a major war the randomness of selection can, in turn, decline until exclusion from service comes down to clear physical disability, or to employment in work considered necessary to the war effort. Once in, enlisted men and officers are slotted into place and made identifiable by their clothes and badges.

Actually there are some nuances here too. Like members of old established families, some top commanders develop a personal style of dress that stretches the limits of uniform. Patton and Montgomery were famous for the highly individual fashion they imposed on prescribed army dress during World War II. Those at the top of the ladder, it seems, can break the rules that demonstrate the power of the hierarchy. Individuality asserts itself as a symbol of ultimate status, but no one lower down had better try that game. What would Field Marshal Montgomery have had to say, one wonders, to a lieutenant wearing a shabby sweater that drooped below his jacket, fur-lined boots, and a black beret?

Celebrities in other areas may also signal their superiority by adopting some kind of noticeable dress, though here too their selections often approach the condition of uniform. Top stars in rock music go in for glitz. They certainly don't look like the ordinary rest of us, though their fans copy them as ardently as their funds permit, but they do look rather like each other: Sparkle has been in since the rise of Liberace, and we expect outrageousness of costume in any public appearance. These celebrities make an interesting group that is clearly serving a function in society: presenting outrageous dress that challenges propriety in an area that is not obviously political. In this it resembles the sort of black humor that acts as a safety valve by diverting opposition toward an aesthetic expression. The people in charge can label this impulse as childish since it doesn't appear to threaten outright, activist rebellion. It's emotionally satisfying but not disruptive in a serious way: its own kind of opium of the people.

Costume codes, then, allow for variation as a sign of top rank, but they must still belong to the range of language for presentation of the self that can be understood in our society. Since clothing is now relatively cheap and social mobility greater, what one wears can be more personally expressive than in the past, but—like language and gesture—it must still fit into a wider frame of reference. If other people can't interpret what one is saying about oneself and one's place in the world, weirdness takes one right off the stage. The label it carries is "mad" or "marginal" at best, and the prescription reads, Keep your distance. Anyone walking the streets of a city today encounters beggars who are identifiable, whether they are accompanied by a dog and wear little signs to announce that they are blind or are offering a packet of pencils for sale and a tin cup in which to deposit money. We know who they are. But we also encounter the disoriented homeless and they have no familiar label or agreed-on rank in the structure at all. They are the disturbing fringe of the underclass and all they can tell us about themselves is that they are indeed distant, outside, unaccountable, and unaccounted for.

There are two things to say about these fringe people. Like those dim figures in the saintly legends who existed as proof of the holiness of the saints, their own experience is taken to have no value at all in the recognized ranks of the hierarchy. These are the alien, and whatever they may know from their experience is so distant that it is irrelevant and can be ignored in planning or managing politics or the economy. Even the good charitable folk who work to help them don't imagine that their lives *as lived* have meaning for others: They are only examples of disaster, cautionary warnings. A hundred years ago, the high-minded English reformers who did their best to succor these outcasts spoke of them as "people of the abyss." They hoped that the rich and great would examine their souls and try to prevent disasters like this from happening in the future, but they did not, could not, credit the idea that these people were like themselves. What gave Shaw's *Pygmalion* its shock value was neither its language nor its jokes about middle-class morality. It was that Eliza, like Cinderella, got to go to the ball; she turned out to be Just Like Us.

Second, by standing visibly outside society as a warning to all, the underclass plays a profoundly important role *in* society. Its message is clearest to those who live close to the bottom, which may be why it is not so clear to those who are farther away. Beggars and vagabonds, deviants and crazies, and unsuccessful small-time criminals all provide menacing evidence of what happens to those who lose the niche granted them by authority. Falling into the quagmire at the foot of the ladder is the threat that keeps those clutching the bottom rungs hanging on. Respectability, once the goal, has lost its attractiveness and Shaw's middle-class morality has vanished behind the Arabian Nights display of *Dallas* and *Dynasty*. But the goal is still being in, being there, on the same vertical map of status as the stars at the top. Television and gossip magazines have taken the place of local chat and tattle, but they provide the same sense of belonging to a social entity.

We put up with a lot to be saved from chaos. We always have.

Chapter 8

POWERFUL PEOPLE GET AWAY WITH THINGS.

That's one way to demonstrate their difference from the rest of us. In *Powers of the Weak* I took as an example of this kind of separation the "trickster-heroes" of myth and legend, the risk takers who break rules and violate taboos and nevertheless escape punishment. Such exploits echo through literature and turn up in tall tales from a hundred different cultural backgrounds, including our own. Davy Crockett, James Bond, MacHeath, and even muscleminded, rule-breaking Rambo belong to their company, and every new season's television shows depict variant clones to suit current moods and modes. We're uneasy about defining these amoral, lively, attractive demigod/monsters. Do they normalize violence and make watchers or readers more likely to use it themselves in daily life? Or do they supply vicarious experience that permits viewers to share condemned behavior without really acting it out? Are they role models for machismo? And if so, is that good, bad, or inevitable?

If we can step back a bit from the argument, which isn't going to be settled until our own attitudes toward violence shift from attraction to boredom, it's possible to see what warning the risk-taking trickster holds for the rest of us. His rule breaking works as a social control. *He* may get away with things, but how do we know that *we* can? Are we ready to match his audacity, overturn custom and face danger, the police, and the wrath of the gods, as he does? In ordinary times, most ordinary people would rather see than be him, would rather sit tight in the niches they have earned for themselves, speak politely, and behave as they are expected to. In terrible times, of course, it might be different; desperation changes a lot. Do these trickster-heroes perhaps preserve an image of mad and thoughtless daring in preparation for some millenarian moments that lie ahead?

In ordinary times, however, the right to violate taboos and break the commandments is reserved to the ultimate power, the state, and the state is jealous. If criminal violence challenges its monopoly, it moves at once to take vengeance. It sets to work the processes that define these lawbreakers— rapists, murderers, thieves, arsonists, terrorists—and it demonstrates the accuracy of the labels by punishment. Only in times of war does the state sanction violence for use by its citizens, as members of armed forces defending the state.

At least, that's what the rules say. But the state is itself a master trickster, and no one knows better how to rewrite rules than those who are charged with doing this as a duty. Indeed, the rules aren't always clearly established even in the minds of the Establishment. Civil disagreement can enlist the state on one side of an argument, and those on that side may find it's easy to bend some rules in their favor. Implementing the law doesn't necessarily follow passing of the law, either. Enforcement varies in the force it can command. And sometimes administrators get their personal ambitions mixed up with the office they hold and assume that official power is theirs to be used for individual whims. Again, the whole Establishment will join hands, or circle the wagons, against a surprised populace in favor of their own clique. Old friends of those in high office can smile their way back to the seats of power and earn good money for doing so from clients who need a rule or two bent. The idea of power as a possession, whose asset value can be banked and drawn on when needed, comes easy to a society whose rules grow out of the methods of finance capitalism.

But in fact power, while it can be used in this way for a

while, is the product of a long-term process of interaction between rulers and ruled. Its purpose is pragmatic, effective management of society as a whole, though in any human world, those who make the most noise at closest range will be heard more clearly than the people at the bottom of the ladder. Myth and history agree that power is used best when the distance between those at the top and those at the bottom can be bridged, when Good Kings or Wise Sultans walk the streets in disguise to hear what's said by the underclass, or when representative democracy works well enough for needs at the bottom to be made known at the top.

That ideal is an ideal of course, a representation of one sort of golden age of small homogeneous communities that may or may not have existed as we imagine them. Even inside such groups some kinds of distancing must have existed: There are always children to be taught, there are always poor relatives or neighbors who make up a "them" that is different from "us." As clans and communities approach the condition of established states, those in power move away from the rest of the citizenry. They may even see themselves as elevated toward the sacred. Their supremacy may be protected not just by law but by the force of taboo, both implicit and explicit. In the long run the distance between rulers and ruled is a high price to pay: The loss of talent and imagination in order to gain mere obedience is a bad bargain. But it's a tempting choice in times of trouble and confusion. It is, of course, a choice that must depend on definition: on labeling, on the assignment of importance to one group above all others, and sometimes to an individual. It has unforeseen consequences too, including the redrawing of maps.

Let us go back a couple of thousand years and look at a famous example of distancing and redefining, the moment when the Roman Republic turned itself into an empire. The "Claudius" novels of Robert Graves and the television series made from them a few years ago acquainted readers and viewers with some of the context of this structural shift. I will concentrate here on the redefinition through which a young Roman general, Octavian, became the emperor Augustus and then was elevated in the public mind to more-than-human status. Celebrated by the most famous poets of the age, he was hailed as a redeemer, the long hoped for herald of a golden age of peace and prosperity. At his death his elevation was made complete: He was deified as Augustus the God.

This apotheosis had been preceded by a troubled age: the decline of the Roman Republic, years of unsettled experiments in government, and wars both foreign and civil. The distressed public (and we have historians as well as poets to speak for them) took what comfort it could in imagining the return of an ancient time when the god Saturn held the reins of power over a land of peace and riches. The vision glowed ever more seductively as the present grew darker and more chaotic. The restoration of the once and future age of gold would be announced, it was believed, by the appearance of a messiah. Christian myth does indeed hold that one was born in just these years, within a small and localized sect; a messiah whose message was decidedly different. But his advent and his fate were hardly known to most Romans for centuries. It was the rise of Augustus from military hero to grand political eminence, who also held the post of Pontifex Maximus (a sort of equivalent of the pope in the state religion) that, combined with public yearning for an end to the insoluble disruption of life, finally gave him the identity of the messiah foretold by Virgil.

Sacred power now separated him from those he ruled, but ruling was still necessary. The distanced public was still demandingly present. The promise of peace and prosperity and fewer laws to interfere with daily life still had to be fulfilled, for raising a secular ruler to supernal heights had not ended the relationship between governor and governed. It did, however, allow authority to rewrite the terms of that relationship. If the ruler had now become a redeemer, likened in powerful verse to Jupiter, king of the gods, then the status of the populace had changed too.

This altered relationship was expressed in a new definition of the public malaise that weighed so heavily on the governed. It was the result of sin, *their* sin; a Roman version of the Fall of Man. Romans had abandoned their ancient traditions of morality and taken to sexual license, and this private misbehavior had a public coordinate. By rejecting traditional values, they were somehow guilty of opposing legitimate government. Political doubts and personal impropriety were joined together. Most people accepted the connection as plausible; poets and historians did too. "For Livy as for Horace," writes historian Andrew Wallace-Hadrill "civil war and immorality are intertwined. War is regarded as the wages of sin: the termination of war is not strictly a military affair, but a religious crusade against sin that results in expiation."[1]

Now the governing member of the political partnership comes to the fore again. Who is to bring about the cure for this terrible disorder? Who can prescribe the penance and provide the forgiveness needed by this multitude of sinners? Why, who else but the messiah, the priest-emperor likened to Jupiter, whose supernatural power is demonstrated and justified by his acts of clemency to the guilty.

Now that the political and moral maps have been redrawn as one, the diagnosis is clear and action can follow. "Sin, whether armed rebellion or sexual misdemeanour, constitutes opposition to authority."[2] Treatment is prescribed accordingly. The sinners must confess their fault and throw themselves on the mercy of the redeemer. We have a record of the appropriate form of words: "I have erred, acted rashly, and I repent. I throw myself on your mercy, beg pardon for the offence, pray that it may be forgiven."[3] In just this form of words Cicero spoke to Caesar Augustus as advocate for the former rebel, Ligurius, begging for his life without any thought of justifying his activities.

For when political misbehavior is transmuted into personal sin, the whole legal system goes by the board. There can be no justification for sin; there can only be forgiveness of what has been laid bare by repentance. Opposition to the ruler has ceased to be a secular political act and become impious, and impiety cannot be explained, only confessed in fear. Dealing with it doesn't require legal redress, it demands the intervention of the Being who represents divine authority. Now the political partnership has dissolved into ultimate power, possessed by One Alone, and those who grovel in hope of mercy. Justice ceases to matter. Action moves outside the temporal world where crime must be proved and judged on the basis of actual evidence. "The emperor stood above the law . . . following his sense of right and wrong, not the law's rigid prescriptions."[4] Sin and crime have got so completely mixed up that politics and morality can no longer be separated from each other.

Such confusion of private and public responsibilities not only validated the position of the emperor-redeemer as standing above all legal constraints; it also laid the blame for pain, suffering, and failure in daily life directly on the shoulders of a guilty populace. "If political crisis was seen as the fault of the Roman people, not the dynasts who competed for power [during the pre-Augustan time of troubles], the way lay open for acceptance of the dynast as the only one who could save the Romans from their own intolerable faults. . . . The solution lay no longer in republican institutions, but in a Messiah."[5]

What had gone wrong? A troubled people, seeking a rationale for proper behavior that would bring some kind of order to a disturbed world, accepted a new map that promised guidance. But the map's prescriptions had unforeseen results. They "explained" the disorder in the world by blaming it on the suffering victims. When authority was elevated toward divine status, it not only separated itself from contact with the ruled but implicitly rejected accountability to them. Accountability demonstrates cause and effect in action. It must fall somewhere, if the universe is to be understandable and daily life to be predictable at all. Since the ruler could no longer be blamed, the cause of trouble must devolve on the other member of the political relationship. Those in trouble, said the logic of this new system, are responsible for their troubles themselves. The prescription to "grin and bear it" had acquired an added clause: "And anyway it's your own fault."

Obviously unpleasant omens for our own times are to be found in these events, beginning with a warning against confusing religion and the state and including a possible corollary, that the only good messiah is a dead messiah. To be ruled by a power so removed that its dictates are beyond reach or argument leads to loss of control over one's life; all rules have become mutable. Morality has eaten up politics, and bargaining over public affairs must now be conducted in a language whose words change their meaning with the will of the ruler. Everyone who turns to authority has to do so individually, asking for favors not justice. The enshrined state confronts a pulverized people made up of single human beings. The needs they feel, their very approach, speaks of a search for grace, not for recognized and established entitlements.

The process by which a successful soldier rose toward the divine power that was formalized at his death (and later bestowed on his living successors) is interesting in itself. Its origin can be traced to the widespread myth of a golden age, which is terribly enticing in any time of trouble. It tends to appear regularly when the present seems so grim that a threatened community turns to dreams in order to nourish a hope that life can be, somehow, sometime, better than it is. Very few radical political movements, whether on the right or on the left, have failed to appeal to yearnings for a better time, an ordered past. Where Romans of the Augustan age were invited by their poets to imagine the return of the great age of Saturn, American conservatives today will themselves into believing in a past of law and order, good behavior growing out of proper family discipline and schoolroom instruction in traditional values. But the conservatives' special demons, Marx and Engels, were also convinced that the roots of communism could be found in an older golden age, that of precapitalist communities. A generation earlier, angry British radicals, confronting the social revolution of industrialization, declared that they were dedicated to restoring the ancient rights of freeborn Englishmen. A century later, Gandhi's spinning wheel symbolized the independent and productive culture of India before the "free-born" British conquerors arrived.

"We did it before, we can do it again." That is the message these mythic memories deliver. They increase the credibility of political leaders who are calling for change. To regain, or remake, a system enjoyed by one's forefathers always seems more feasible then inventing one from scratch, while it also plays on a national, or ethnic, chauvinism. In addition it provides a target for natural anger: the usurpers who took away ancient rights and customs. Though, as we have seen, the target may be shifted, in the end to those who are simply hoping for better times.

Unfortunately the kind of past that hearsay and selective memory recall, or that charismatic propagandists offer the public, is legendary rather than historical. It's a past enshrouded in myths. They make it familiar, and familiarity helps to confirm our belief in the definitions that we're offered, but it doesn't make them true. Traditions and legends are persuasive just because they supply simplified versions of what happened, distorted by what we want to think happened. They gloss over contradictions and suppress reports on what went wrong.

History, after all, is always being rewritten. It's vulnerable to redefinition according to the priorities of a particular age, this present or that one, ours or our ancestors' or our descendants'. When we turn to history looking for answers to contemporary problems, we envision our needs and judge the solutions offered according to the intellectual and emotional preconceptions of our time. The answers, that is, must fit the questions we ask.

The most plausible answers are influenced by myth, just because myth suppresses the general human confusion that history shows. It does so in order to hang together and give us answers that will stop our asking awkward questions about factual contradictions, about the relevance of records, about how to interpret them according to today's priorities. But that doesn't mean that the past, both mythic and historical, isn't relevant. If we ask the right questions, we may, in fact, discover useful data not only about what happened then that fits our present-day questions, but also about the ways in which human minds and emotions work when we/they look at the world around.

In Augustan Rome, authority redefined itself in order to increase its control over a threatening situation. Redefining the duties, and the nature, of the lesser partner in politics followed: Prescriptions for behavior were thus laid down. We have also noted the redefinition, and the directives, that sought to place freed black slaves in the United States and the Caribbean. An even more dramatic and demanding call for definition confronted the European conquerors who originally burst into the New World of the Americas. Here was a totally unknown stretch of territory, enormous and varied, inhabited by humans whose customs, languages, and cultures were utterly alien. How were a handful of invaders going to identify what they found and explain it to themselves well enough to deal with these mysterious strangers? In Central America, after all, the conquistadors came upon functioning, civilized societies, not just a handful of savages appearing and disappearing in a howling wilderness who could easily be seen as akin to animals.

Can we imagine ourselves back into the situation of those who discovered new territories that figured on no maps, and new societies that fitted no preconceptions, a world that had never been imagined in all the centuries of history? It was an experience closer to those invented by writers of science fiction than any projected by early social philosophers. Indeed, enough science fiction has been written to prepare us, today, for such an eventuality. Our ancestors, however, faced the unsettling knowledge that their records, and their vision of life in the existing world, was and always had been inaccurate. Here was a whole great landmass that they knew nothing about, one that teemed with animals, plants, men and women with their own multifarious ways of living that neither the sages of the past nor the prophets in the Bible had ever hinted at. How was it that they were not bowled over by their ignorance?

In the absence of knowledge, says historian Michael Ryan,[6] these invaders turned to concepts that afforded the comfort of familiarity. In the first place, the Renaissance had been making its own discoveries of a past that was more than mythic. Classical texts, increasingly available as the printing press reproduced them, spoke of high cultures existing centuries earlier that were diverse among themselves as well as different from the world of the sixteenth century. Awareness of such texts dimmed the intellectual shock of coming on an alien universe. At least the possibility of diversity was familiar, although this particular diversity was strange.

That abstract answer, however, didn't deal with pragmatic necessity: How was one actually to cope with, not just chaos waiting to be sorted out and labeled, but a structured unknown system that operated by its own indecipherable rules? Authority is more sensitive to shame than the rest of us. It's terribly visible, and so mistakes by those who stand at the top of the ladder of hierarchy have a wider circulation and are remembered longer than the blunders of the rest of us, down below. Proper behavior is important to authority in a very acute sense, and it depends on knowing that one particular action will call forth a particular response. How can one know this in a universe of strangers? Who *are* these people? Are they dangerous and if so, what kind of danger are they likely to be planning? Currently our science fiction writers seem to imagine that invaders in their spaceships will arrive with a good deal of advance information about the inhabitants of the planet Earth. That was not the situation of our forefathers when they stumbled on the New World.

So they were fortunate in having not only Renaissance recoveries of the classical past to call on, but also a second line of mental defense inherited from the early Middle Ages and the writings of the Church fathers. This second map not only supplied an awareness of unfamiliar worlds; it suggested appropriate action. These strange folk could and should be labeled "pagans." The proper approach was to convert them to Christianity, just as Saints Cyril and Methodius had converted the Slavs and Saint Augustine the Angles and Saxons, and just as the pagan Northman, Rolf, had converted himself into Rollo, the Christian Norman and founder of a European dynasty. True, these newfound pagans exhibited startling customs, styles of life, religious practices, and degrees of civilization. But the devil, it was well known, was skillful in deception and inventive of ingenious evils; so said the Christian fathers. "A body of demonological theory ... could provide the ethnographer with the conceptual tools for understanding the otherwise inexplicable, often terrifying, behavior of exotic peoples ... shamanic trances ... strange nocturnal disturbances ... religious cruelties."[7] An old map that made "otherness" nameable absorbed and naturalized these strangers and prescribed not only conversion but also the prompt destruction of all written or pictorial records of their practices. They were works of the devil! Into the fire, then, with this puzzling material evidence of difference, and into the arms of the Church with those who could now be relabeled as a familiar sort of "them."

If, when we encounter strangers, we can pin a known

tag on them, it's a relief. They've been placed on a map we've seen before and have lost the threat of danger they carried. But our relief has less to do with the strangers, whoever they are, than with our own anxieties. Definitions should end with prescriptions for action by the defined of course, but also with directions for effective, coping action by the definers. The latter, needless to say, are the most important for the definers. These actions should serve their interests and make them comfortable mentally. Once that's done, the people in charge can get on with their business of being in charge without having to stop to think what to do next. Now there are rules for proper behavior on the part of both definers and defined. If the rules are accepted, well and good. Then authority knows what to expect. If the governed don't agree, not so good, but still good enough as long as any misconduct can be contained or minimized by labeling them as children, or by distancing them as others. Then they can be controlled through techniques of shaming and stigmatization, by legalized enforcement, or by economic sanctions that will counter efforts at rebellion.

It's true that in the case of casual encounters the existence of strangers may produce no definitions at all. Since labeling is done for the convenience of Us, the Powerful, it is done only when we feel that some sort of relationship exists and must be recognized as present. Unless "they" are important enough to "us" to need a label and acquire a role, we'd never bother with them. Traveling abroad, we can be amused by the odd behavior of foreigners and their quirky languages as long as their outlandish carryings-on take place in a public space where we can keep our distance. The people we take the trouble to define are the ones who impinge on our world, and whose presence there is going to continue.

Thus Augustus, who could only be emperor of the Romans, after all, by recognizing the existence of the Romans, devised a new code of behavior, through which a universal stigma was accepted and atonement sought. The myth of a golden past became so compelling that his subjects were seized with a sincere desire to renounce the evil habits that had corrupted their lives and consequently destroyed the serene days and ways of old. They had to be born again, confess and ask forgiveness for sin. Sexual license was seen as a threat against order and equated with rebellion against the state. The Ayatollah Khomeini has followed the pattern closely, and Muslim fundamentalism is rising throughout the Arab lands and beating on the foundations of the political establishments there.

Thus also the Christian conquerors of what they blithely misnamed the Indies dealt with their own confusion over the diversity of differences they found there by lumping these aliens together under the label "pagans" and setting up a role for themselves as missionaries bringing truth and light to the heathen. True, they could not count on these pagans to accept the label given them since it came out of an unfamiliar past. But another process that they imported to the Americas helped their campaign: European disease, hitherto unknown in the New World, prevented successful revolt by killing off the native population. This genocide-by-accident, so to speak, could be seen (if it was seen at all) as placing these aliens in a category of impotence. The casual devastation brought by the invaders could be read as a sign of the power of themselves and their God.

A dream I had while I was struggling with the first draft of this chapter supplies a symbolic dream-weird image of just this kind of external redefinition. Someone else (perhaps the ghost of Hernando Cortez) and I were together in a large, dark, rather formal house. Loose in it were several wild animals that we were trying to shut up before they became aware that they could destroy us if they chose to. Again and again we managed to herd them into some inner room and slam the door, but it did no good. They always found a way out. Until, that is, we confined each of them inside the polished shell of a giant turtle! Then the bull and the tiger and the huge dog were caged in the dress of another species (one vaguely appropriate to Central America, too, in my sleeping mind), and they became tameable: Mayas, Incas, Aztecs, and all, defined as pagans, each bundled into a category of otherness that had nothing at all to do with their own essential being. It was a way to deal with *our* fear by confining *them* in disabling armor.

I seldom trust my dreams to deliver open, straightforward messages, but this one may have been reinforced by my own need to define the ideas I was trying to get onto paper (though I very much hope I have not misrepresented them so drastically!). But the lumping together of unfamiliar entities into a category is a ubiquitous psychological tool. Come back for a moment to the prescribing doctor, labeling a disease as the first step to dealing with those sleepless nights, that terrible rash. How much dare we trust his identification of our trouble if he begins by lumping it into a category?

Good doctors seem to worry about that. Here is one describing the problem of coping with a multisymptomed disorder, schizophrenia. Silvano Arieti wrote a lengthy book about this malady. Reading it, one feels that his work may have been powered by a need to convince himself as well as his readers that such labeling was justified at all. Could the ranges of behavior described here (and they are fascinating and revealing of psychological processes in general) actually be joined together under one label? For the patient suffering from this condition reveals it by wildly original behavior and language, imagery that is odd to the point of uniqueness. How can such extreme difference be labeled as similar to anything else in the world? Arieti is asking. And yet it must somehow be named and placed on a map if the doctor is going to be able to do what doctors have been invented to do, cope with illness. Arieti writes:

It's true that we view schizophrenics as being similar to one another, and we are able to detect common symptoms in them. It is because of these common symptoms that we are able to recognize them. Actually their realm of originality exceeds by far that of the normal man. Paradoxically they seem similar to us because they are original and because they do not use our methods of thinking. They are similar in their difference from us, just as all Chinese may appear similar to Caucasians. Being unable to understand the originality of the content of their expressions and actions, we tend to emphasize the frequent occurrence of the few formal mechanisms that we understand. Paradoxically, it is by adopting universal *forms that the individuality of the patient, with its specific dynamic determinants, is allowed to emerge.*[8] *(Arieti's emphasis)*

Coping with the specificity of madness by bundling it into a category that can be identified only by its difference from norms is a revealing clue to authority's urge to define and to the common human need to know ourselves and to be known. Our behavior, more than spoken language, identifies us and prevents misunderstanding. Children avoid this risk because they are labeled as learners who will obey rules once they can grasp them. Rebels reject traditional patterns by deliberate decision. But the pitiful, dangerous mad are denied any place in the network of agreed-on significance that unites the rest of us in a community. That calamity is frightening. How can we be sure that it will never happen to us?

In times of great change the task of defining grows heavy. Society itself must be reshaped as relationships, private and public, alter. They must be judged according to unfamiliar circumstances and reinterpreted as normal, childish, rebellious, or crazy. The power structure is under pressure to fulfill the duty that it claims, to order the lives of all of us, the powerful included, and to do so in the face of an upsurge of behavior whose derivation and purpose are mysterious. A need to control and a need to understand these breaks with convention contend with each other. So it was for the Roman Establishment attempting to structure a system whose size and complexity were brand-new. So it is today for old and new imperialists and for the former subjects of European invaders, who are suddenly in revolt against a culture whose erstwhile attraction vanished with its power. The retreat of the West has initiated a desperate search for plausible directives that can predict events and prescribe ways of coping with them; and that's true of the West as well as its former subjects. All of it has happened before, over and over. That knowledge provides very little comfort to anybody.

So authority, somewhat reconstructed itself, begins to sketch out again the maps of relations and causalities that it considers important. There they stand encoded, the seven deadly sins and the cardinal virtues, morals and manners outlined in handbooks for the ambitious, Mrs. Beaton's rules of household management, dress codes and sumptuary laws to prevent the merely rich from aping their betters, the protocols of precedence and of court etiquette. They are supposed to map the world but what they actually chart is the mentality of the powerful. Response, criticism, feedback of some kind, that's what the rest of us provide. We do it best by the active, visible behavior that, as the proverb says, speaks louder than words. But it takes a while to grow brave enough to persist in challenging definitions, and meanwhile authority is reaching for useful new patterns of thought that begin, of course, with their own purposes.

Augustan Rome reestablished the ancient figure of the divine ruler who could not (by definition) be blamed for the hardships of his subjects. It was they who were guilty. The Nazis took a different tack. They too wanted scapegoats for Germany's difficulties, but general guilt was not the answer: The Treaty of Versailles had already laid that burden on the nation, and the Germans were in revolt against it. Hitler and his minions had to redirect the burden away from the German folk. An underlying tradition of anti-Semitism set up the Jews as a natural target, although other alien groups, like the Gypsies, were also used. The accepted suspicion felt for the Jews as wandering, mysterious strangers and the ease with which their difference from "good Germans" could be emphasized, however, gave them prime place. It also blurred the full scope of the policy for "final solution." If the Jews were accepted as alien enough to be persecution worthy, that view screened the step onward that made them murder worthy. A similar attitude has been at work, half in public and half underground, in contemporary South Africa; any despised group can fall further from the level of acknowledged fellowship in the true human race to the point where treating them inhumanly is justified.

As a contemporary of Augustus wrote, "The descent to hell is easy" once you begin. And yet he himself didn't disapprove the advent and the policies of that messiah, he predicted his coming and he supported him with passion: illustrating his own words.

Chapter 9

IF HISTORY REALLY IS RELEVANT

in today's world, the proposition doesn't command much respect. Perhaps the past is a different country, but if so no one much wants to travel there. Even the personal histories of living people get lost as their circumstances change and, like chameleons, they change too. "You've come a long way," is a very American compliment, which is also a compliment to the speaker. Those who are being praised illustrate the value of American goals and customs by their determination to succeed American style. Those who offer praise make clear the expertise that licenses them to judge the newcomers' ability to survive and to profit from the melting pot.

Historically speaking, losing the past began long ago in the New World and the melting-pot label well described the process by which old customs were, and were expected to be, forgotten. For individuals, the transatlantic crossing all but guaranteed the disappearance of the structure on which ties of community had been based. Some ties were preserved out of need, but as an act of will, not nature. There was little support for them in the American ethos of competition or the American practice of moving on. Other immigrants arrived as members of the utopian groups that were dedicated in advance to creating new structures for living. Puritans and Quakers, Mennonites and Owenites, Moravians and Old Believers, like the native-born who swelled the ranks of Mother Ann's Shaker communities and those who found new light in Mormon revelations (which in fact attracted many immigrants), had no desire to reestablish the Old World's social patterns of rank.

In any case, whether by choice or by force of circumstances, life in new conditions was so demanding and the need to adapt so imperative that public traditions vanished quickly. After all, if the newcomers had been happily ensconced where they were they would hardly have taken the trouble to move. Later, certainly, pride in their roots and in their ethnic heritage surfaced, but by that time accurate memories of the old country, whichever old country it might be, had begun to soften. Survival almost demands it and adjustment to change enforces it. Who wants to dwell on the hardness of hard times, day to day, minute to minute, beaten into the flesh and the mind? Add to personal pain the impossibility of conveying these memories to children who never knew such a life and will judge it as strangers, terrified and shamed by a vision of their parents caught in complexities and conflicts whose pressures can't be made clear and are, hope the survivors, now irrelevant. In the same way, social and geographical mobility within the United States has bred a sentimentalized version of small-town life and happy days on the family farm that is not terribly factual. Americans, new and old, must indeed have cherished a belief in progress to shed history so fast. All of us, it seems, have gone through the melting pot.

None of that would matter much if we had not imported our foreshortened and falsified vision of the past into our view of the world as it is and should be. Like it or not, we can't re-create the Good Old Days since the social and economic infrastructure that sustained them no longer exists; but if we distort them and their values, we're inviting confusion. The human race does indeed retreat toward mythic solutions in hard times, and as a source of strength and emotional support they can be valuable. But as guidelines for action these prescriptions are polluted with some element, large or small, of wish fulfillment. They make past struggles seem easy, even inevitable. They deny the losses and costs of what was finally gained and ignore the inge-nious solutions that resolved some problems and the endurance and courage that subdued others. Nonetheless we feel uneasily that we have lost something we could use in order to place ourselves, something that might help us draw new maps that would hold steady in the face of uncertainty.

For how can we even reach the goal of staying up-to-date when we can't judge the importance of what's going on around us? Current social shifts seem unplanned and incoherent and their meanings elusive. Last year's answers won't solve our problems without our having to wrestle with them, think them through, and test possible courses for action.

That's authority's business, of course, but doing it quickly short-circuits the creative process and invites the use of ready-made concepts that can be adapted to fit an awkward situation. The myth of a golden age, universally attractive, can be exploited in a variety of ways. One handy technique is the invention of new traditions that seem to provide connections with a colorful if specious past. The same impulse, "to make it old," moves universities to plant ivy around the foundations of raw brick buildings. The impression of antiquity conveys the suitability of what is done and taught there; no one is then invited to ask "How old is old?" and thus to question the legitimacy of visible authority.

The invention of tradition has a respectable past of its own. Eric Hobsbawm, the English historian, has edited a collection of reports on invented tradition in the British Isles and in some of her colonies over the last century and a half. Some of them were imposed from without, as in India and Africa, while others fed romantic exercises in nationalism among the Scots and the Welsh. Whatever the setting, the technique defined proper roles to be played by those who took these inventions on faith. In Africa, writes Terence Ranger, a mix of several English traditions drawn from the army, from public schools, and from the relationship of masters and servants in great houses were "made use of to create a clearly defined hierarchical society in which Europeans commanded and Africans accepted command."[1] These directions for proper behavior employed the African tradition of kingship to present the constitutional British monarch in the same guise:

In Northern Rhodesia the chiefs played up to the official "theology" by addressing their requests for guns or uniforms to the king through his governor and sent the king presents of leopard skins or tusks; African dance associations elected their kings and Kaisers to preside over them with proper ceremony; millenarian preachers told their audiences that King George, who had hitherto been deceived by his corrupt advisors, would assume direct control and usher in the golden age.[2]

Such wholesale redrawing of maps and creation of novel conceptual structures did not establish a long-lasting system, especially when it was imposed from outside. It did, however, destroy the political and economic infrastructure of many indigenous systems of thought, so that when the imported maps faded away, there were gaps in the picture of the universe as seen by ex-subjects of imperialist rulers. By distorting independent visions of connected reality, of cause and effect, and of proper behavior for managing existence, the incursive Europeans had discredited the experience of the original inhabitants even when they used native traditions. Those traditions had been twisted, if not uprooted. A re-creation of proper styles for living that will incorporate roots of the past and connect them with today's demands now falls on the shoulders of the inheritors, and it's no minor task that they face.

A rejection of alien rule and its concepts is not among the difficulties that Americans and western Europeans confront, but shifts in daily experience at all levels have probably had comparable effects. The traditions we received from our ancestors—what we recall of them—have lost their capacity to explain what's going on and to tell us how to deal with events. What we do recall is mostly generalities, since the details of ordinary life, the data that gave rise to generalities, have disappeared. We have some of the superstructure but not the particulars and the processes on which it was built. If we are going to be able to judge the value of traditions, as recalled, to contemporary life, we need to know something about the facts, the pressures, and the premises that were extant and relevant in the days when the traditions were born.

For that we must turn again to history, which prides itself on dealing in facts. Of course interpretations differ and new material is always being added to the archives, but history is what can be documented: the present as it used to be, as it was written down by people of different kinds, all of them different in some degree from us. No doubt we'll misunderstand much of these records and should be ready to read with imaginative openness, but we won't be tempted to misinterpret them mindlessly by assuming that our ancestors were just like us and would have come to the same conclusions that we would reach. Instead, if we look hard and ask patiently, we may be able to come closer to what they naturally thought. Then the dry-as-dust documents take on some life. We have annals and court reports, journals, registers of births and deaths, lists of ships built and commissioned and ships lost; we have logs of their voyages and letters home from foreign parts, ambassadors' reports, account books of merchants and banks, and beginning as soon as records were kept we have lists of taxes due and taxes paid. The Domesday Book that told William the Conqueror just what he had conquered, the Landnamabok that recorded the farms and their boundaries taken up by the Vikings who came into Iceland, the minutes of debates in Congress and Parliament—all these exist and are open to questions, which can be repeated in the light of changing circumstances. We can learn and we can correct ourselves.

Of course a lot of what has come down to us in the documents we rely on and much that has been written about it concerns itself with history as seen by the great: battles and victories and royal marriages and contention between the Church and the Crown, and so on. As political systems took account of more than the people at the top, regular history broadened its base too. But only rather recently have historians given substantial thought and time to the lives and activities of the citizenry, areas where tradition and folktale had been the repositories of experience. The last few decades, however, have witnessed an explosion of research and publication in social history that has wrung out many legends that were taken for granted, and which some historians feel, now needs to be pruned a bit itself. However that may be, we have gained enormously in the range of what we can think about seriously in realistic terms.

Within social history itself, lost areas have been rediscovered with the growth of black history and women's history, fields where legend had absorbed actuality almost completely, since the lives of their native dwellers had been granted little importance. Here the nongreat were seen en masse and seen frequently, sometimes romantically, as "others." Reclaiming their experience, to the extent that it can be done without ourselves falling into wish fulfillment, changes history by adding weight and context to standard political reports. When Henry Ford remarked, some sixty-odd years ago, that "history is bunk," he might well have meant that too much was left out. Little was being written then about engineering progress and invention and Ford must certainly have felt that royal marriages were pretty uninteresting in comparison to the development of technology and what it meant for the lives of ordinary people. Today the history of technology and of its social consequences has many practitioners.

Such workaday experience was recorded without any thought of its value for the future. Letters and journals, recipes, wills, and contracts help us to see and to feel the shape of the past as it appeared to those who lived there: what they took to be important, the rules that seemed unbreakable and also the resentment and misbehavior those rules could provoke, the goals that could be conceived and worked for because they were possible and not simply fantasies, and of course the yearly round of work and pastimes that filled past time. It's not tradition, so often prettied and gentrified, that can show us what it is we have actually lost that might be valuable if we could reinvent an up-to-date version; it's the immediacy of real life. Unless we can sense the humanness of those long-gone folk, their pain and pleasure, their anger and joy, and something of what their myths meant to them, not us, we are missing a vital chance for understanding ourselves. Certainly human nature changes in its concepts and practices, but it doesn't change in absolutely incomprehensible ways. Maps for behavior have a genealogy just as people do.

So even when we begin to redraw old maps, we do not want to throw the originals away out of hand. As any dedicated closet cleaner knows, clearing out debris can be exhilarating, but occasionally we throw away things that we will miss later and whose loss we regret. Then we may overvalue what's gone and in so doing overlook items that still don't seem important. "Traditional values" have gone through two sorts of reevaluation in the last generation, from the intoxication with the new of the 1960s to the efforts of the 1980s to return us to a past where old iniquities and inequities are dismissed. Both responses have failed to take account adequately of shifts in the physical world: including the transformation of cities to megalopolises; the demographics of population growth, especially through immigration and the drastic economic realignment in which industry and jobs have moved from old to new settings; and the altered social structures that have resulted from these changes.

I realize that the injunction, Look at history, is not very useful in itself as a way of surmounting the culture shock that has been labeled "future shock." Well, of course the central purpose for writing this book is my belief that unraveling the techniques of definition can help us discover where to look and what to look for. These techniques grow out of the psychology both of individuals and of the social groups in which they live. They lie below the surface of conscious existence, and their operations are more permanent than any that are intentionally devised. They underscore the continuity of power relationships and social requirements and the political interlocking of the two. Any kind of government depends on its ability to develop and demonstrate common purpose, agreed to by the governed majority and thus making the policies of the powerful legitimate. Agreement of the citizenry with these definitions and prescriptions depends on their plausibility, on their fit with the perceptions and hopes of ordinary people as they are felt at any particular time. I think of this intertwined process as "the rules of the game," inevitably present in any society and inevitably at work to adjust society to inevitable changes in the physical world and in the economic structure and just as inevitably influenced by the premises of culture and language and religion current in that society. Let me add that the rules seem to me useful for analysis, not for prophecy. But when we have to think ahead, analysis that can define our present position is desperately needed. Analysis depends on asking questions about what we take for granted. If I bring anything new to this quest, it's a concern for the way in which the power to define is at work. It's a universal component of power, and successful power centers know this almost by instinct. Understanding their operations is pretty important for the rest of us too, as a basis for independent judgment.

So the prescription, Look at history, means to suggest that before we fall for traditions, *or* throw them out entirely, we should consider them in terms of the situation in which they came to birth and decide how close it seems to our own situation, and therefore how useful these definition/prescriptions for behavior are apt to be for us.

When we look back at the examples from history of definition that were given in Chapter 8, we can see the conditions out of which they grew: Something had happened to the social machinery in Rome, already an imperium in being, which forced the invention of a new kind of ruler-governor. Even more disastrous for the Aztec polity was the failure of Moctezuma's warriors to contain the Spanish invasion. In the vacuum of power that resulted, the invaders could maintain themselves only if they took command. In both cases the immediate need for order produced violent and corrupt totalitarian rule, prolonged in the New World by the great social and cultural distance between the powerful and the governed. This lesson from history is negative but sadly familiar. The need for a central structure of power can't be denied but the more we know about standard operating rules for managing political realities the more we should be able to avoid the waste that alienation within a society produces.

As things stand, the risks involved in managing the world make most of us decidedly timid and leave us with the feeling that supreme rule had better be handed to someone else. So when we scan the past for guidance in present difficulties, we do well to begin with ordinary events and daily doings. In fact, though they seem closer to our own experiences, they are not separate from great issues but part of an interactive whole that gives human meaning to political disputes. Day-to-day events are easier to get hold of than are matters of state, even though we live very different lives from those of our predecessors of a century ago. Who in the world can care about the causes of wars over the succession to a throne of this or that monarch—aside from a graduate student in history sweating out a dissertation? The occasions for religious strife are even more mysterious. And the awesome potential for disaster that nuclear weapons provides moves the whole definition of "war" to an area known to the past in a quite different context. The end of the world, our ancestors assumed, might be the result of widespread human sin but it would come about through divine intervention or, according to some religions, through cyclical time processes unreachable by human beings. Our own fear, guilt, and powerlessness in the face of a process whose operations are known in detail reduces past scenarios of apocalypse to curious products of alien cultures that have nothing to say to us about our own situation. Daily life, however, is something we can envisage and, with imagination, evaluate.

All right, where do we begin? Today, we're told, the advanced nations are fast becoming an interconnected and interdependent "service economy." In terms of lived experience that simply means that more of us make a living by dealing with people instead of things. We know that smokestack industry is no longer a big employer. Heavy production has either been superseded by advanced technology or exported to "backward" parts of the world because their backwardness supplies international companies with cheap labor and low taxes. What remains of heavy industry and manufacturing produces objects, components of objects, or the material from which objects are made: the "goods" part of the "goods and services" for which people get paid.

The services that earn incomes involve doing things for other people. Of course many of them require the use of goods to a greater or lesser extent. We couldn't have a communications sector of industry without telephones, television, radio, and the ever-present computer, nor could other services from banking to advertising get on without them. But these up-to-date "things" are very complex and incorporate a lot of mental servicing. Their "thinginess" is minor in relation to the amount of service that they require to exist and to deliver services to human beings. They are physical expressions of human talents for dealing with human needs in order to serve these needs.

The higher we climb in the social hierarchy the less likely are people to be actually making or growing *things*. They may manage the making of things, but that means managing the people who make them, and they may simply be managing servicers: insurance executives or newspaper publishers. Again, they may be consultants and adjuncts and facilitators, lawyers and public relations advisers and lobbyists. If they project or supervise the use of things, as engineers and architects still do, they rarely handle the things themselves. Doctors don't dispense medicine anymore, they leave that to pharmacists, and pharmacists increasingly hand out what comes ready-made and ready-mixed from the pharmaceutical companies.

The increasing importance of services at the expense of growing or making things has had a number of results, many of them very valuable. Low prices and availability of consumer goods have revolutionized our standards of comfort, health, and life-span. But other results are less positive. One of them, often bemoaned though without much effort to keep it alive, is the loss of crafts and hand-skills, the old ways of making things. Few of them survive except as hobbies, and the point of hobbies is that while they're rewarding to the hobbyist, they aren't necessary. Whatever we have lost with ceasing to make things by hand is not going to be made good by going back to handicrafts, and crying over it is sheer nostalgia.

But that doesn't mean that something real and important wasn't lost, and its vanishing has had repercussions we overlook in the way that we now connect with the physical world. Let's take a look at some central, experiential effects of what has gone. Our ancestors certainly controlled and shaped physical nature in a much more personal way than we do. Their skills were often reflected in their bodies: One of Sherlock Holmes's notable tricks was to guess the trade or profession of a client by posture or stance or physical evidence of regular work habits shown by calloused hands or worn boots. Work with things leaves its mark on bodies. It leaves marks on minds too. An intimate sort of relationship develops and may continue to deepen as responses to the work's demands continue to increase. The kind of work that our rural ancestors (those semianimal peasants) pursued involved the natural world directly, whereas now machinery intervenes. *We* run equipment. *They* worked with living creatures and growing crops, and the relationships, renewed and enforced every day, shaped their experience and their ways of seeing the world. We have records, and also word-of-mouth descriptions of some of these relationships, culled over the last forty or fifty years as their imminent disappearance made them seem worth reporting for the sake of human archaeology. Here, for example, is a sheep farmer from Scotland training a sheep dog. Most of our dogs today are pets; this one, a border collie, is learning to be a partner in a very important work relationship.

I select a puppy from intelligent parents.... I feed [him] well and give him cod liver oil.... Then comes the hard part. He loves you now and is all over you... but he has to learn to stay away from you and it is against his whole nature. You start by getting him to stay still at five yards, then you walk a little farther—"Now, Ben, sit down— sit!" You are taking the frolic out of him and putting the confidence in.... When you come to work on the sheep and you can stop them (high short whistle) and make them absolutely still from a distance, then you are getting somewhere.[3]

That is just the beginning, of course. All the specific training, the teaching of obedience to commands and of the necessary emotional sense that the dog must learn to handle the sheep properly—"all the time he must be quiet and gentle ... never to worry them, you understand"[4]—is just one segment of many related activities. For the sheep themselves must be kept in good heart, the wool clip gathered and packed, the animals turned out in the right pastures at the right time, the lambing season planned for, all as part of an interconnected system.

There were also the horsemen who handled the plough teams, the dairymaids who milked and made cheese, the hedgers and ditchers, the reapers with their scythes:

*The mowers used their own scythes and were very particular about
them ... it wasn't the buying of them, it was the keeping them
sharp. ... Some men moved so quick they just fled through the corn all
the day long. Each mower took eleven rows of corn on his blade, no
more and no less.*[5]

After harvest came threshing:

*The threshing floor was made within the large barn, usually set be-
tween doors ... so that a through draft could be obtained ... and a
good light. ... The floor would be of beaten earth, smooth and
flat. ... The sheaves of corn were laid in the center ... and the threshers stood round in a ring.*

*... [A] team of threshers might contain as many as eight or ten.
The action was a swinging stroke that made ... the loose end of the
flail swing around behind the head and brought the head of the staff
down on the floor at the end of the stroke. ... The resistance of the corn
and the bounce of the [flail] made a ... shaking motion that loosened
the corn and shook it out.*[6]

With ten flails flying, this was dangerous work. Perfect
time and perfect rhythm had to be kept, and that was done
by the leader who called the changes, often in a chant; just as
the shared interaction of work aboard ship was kept in time
and proper rhythm by sea chanties. What did physical repetition of this kind mean to minds? Boredom? Perhaps, but
the sheer necessity for it must have brought in other meanings too, which had to do with ways of measuring time, with
interdependence and regular sequences of movement. Impulse, one imagines, was downplayed.

No doubt different skills produced different mind-sets,
but all of them—those of the thatcher and his helper, the
blacksmith and his apprentice at the forge, the drovers
walking beside the slow but almost unstoppable oxteams, the
spinners and weavers, the experts who carved the millstones,
the woodcutters and sawyers, beekeepers and poulterers,

stonemasons, brewers, tanners and leather workers—all of them certainly provided a very intimate, in-the-body sense of competence and of continuity. It's easy for us to imagine that the repetitious automatic work turned the workers into automatons. That appears to be an oversimplification. It was the pressure of demands from feudal overlords and from the state, forcing incessant overwork through the threat of starvation, that narrowed minds and shortened lives. In the bad times of the early twentieth century, Ronald Blythe records how sheer pride in their expertise maintained the self-respect of underpaid farm laborers in England.[7] The destruction of the machinery that devalued their skills and did away with their jobs by the Luddites, and the bitter resistance to changes in agricultural methods by the peasantry, did not arise from primitive minds or a stubborn clinging to old ways. It was due to the loss of the means of existence, of whatever poor income could be earned, that the masses of people experienced as the outcome of "improvement."

Long-standing restrictions around apprenticeship to a trade or a craft don't illustrate the mental limitations of master craftsmen, but the value of the skills they commanded. The right to pursue a craft, enforced by membership in a guild, was still seen as equivalent to property.

If opponents of mechanization behaved improperly—and they certainly did, in the eyes of employers and landlords—it was as a way of protecting an entitlement that, being personal, was felt to outweigh the ownership of land or of the nonhuman means of production. A good worker had acquired this right by an expertise whose value was demonstrated over and over. It supported confidence in the possessor's capacity to interact with the environment, physical, animal and human, including the ability to work with others as part of a team. Pride in one's expertise was validated by habit. The personal involvement of our ancestors with making and handling the actual universe, whether that universe was grounded in the land or in the knowledge that we would think of today as being professional—copying manuscripts, planning and supervising construction, managing forests and fisheries—added a dimension to their lives that has now become much less common and significant.

The value of physical expertise, as a trusted part of one's personal resources, lives on today in the arts and in the most widespread and popular art of all, sports; but it falls outside daily existence for most of us. It has been built into the machines that now do skilled work and no doubt do it more efficiently and far faster but that never permit elements of personal choice and direction, the fluid responses to human imagination, that used to be part of craft skills.

I don't mean to sentimentalize what we have lost with the advent of machines or belittle the advances they have brought. Not only are we richer and healthier and longer-lived; our world has widened enormously, our choices would seem incredible to those who lived more than a century ago, and our actions are freer. But it is foolish to ignore what we *have* lost, for if we hope to reclaim old values for new uses, we must first identify them. One important loss, I believe, was exactly the close connection between using specific physical skills and the individual adept and, often, teacher of skills. Not much that I know of has been done to study the physical interaction of hand and brain or of brain and muscular balance and their interplay, but these links must lie very deep since they became automatic and I suspect that they have a place in the sense of self that every individual develops and carries through life.

A special kind of distancing has superseded this connection to the world of things, and it involves the loss of a sense of process: of the time and the skill and the forethought that are needed to accomplish a desired goal. Making a physical object has become a machine job that usually takes place even before the purchaser of the object comes into view, so that its acquisition is all but instant. Unfortunately, however, and especially unfortunate in a service society, nothing has happened to shorten the time needed to establish personal relationships with other human beings, so that we know them and their desires and the quirks and whimsicalities of their personalities and, equally, so that we are willing to trust them with our personal emotional maps. There's a division between our experience of getting what we want in the matter of things and what we want from people. The first experience habituates us to assume that acquiring what we want from people should also be a quick job. If we can get fast food, why shouldn't we get fast love?

Frivolous though the question may sound it's not easy to answer. Habituation to getting things fast is as effective as any kind of habit training. Waiting for satisfaction, as every parent knows, is something that has to be taught and learned. It was easier to learn when all the things people got took quite a time in the getting—in the growing or the making, and were often part of a systematic schedule of operations. The year, every year, went around from ploughing through sowing, hoeing, reaping, threshing, and proper storing of grain or other crops; while before your grain could feed you, there must come milling to flour, bread making, and baking. Patience had to be labeled a virtue where nothing was instant, except perhaps disaster: fire, or flood or war. And in that case patience became a tool for survival.

Awareness of process time, not clock time, produced other psychological effects. Anticipation went with patience. Did it deepen pleasure when the goal was finally reached? Poets seemed to think so. Did knowing that making and growing had to pass through a series of stages give the accomplishment of each stage its own value on the way to the final achievement? The satisfaction of creation has been spoken of often, the pride in doing well and making well and knowing that the work would last and continue to be judged as good. Some of that may have been illusory or exaggerated, it's hard to tell. But if we turn to the remaining areas where skills still count, in sports, we surely see evidence of joy in doing; and in art, joy in making.

Let me say again, these pleasures were offset by misery

and drudgery, by pain and hunger and sickness, by poverty and crippling and shortened lives. We don't want them back at that price. But if the pleasures were real, we have to accept that too. I think there's no doubt that their loss does flatten existence, because we have lost with them a knowledge of life's growth and complexity and of our own potentiality for working with such complex reality so that we control it by interaction and necessarily involve and invest our emotions in our work. A "service economy" that works with people ought to be able to involve us in the same way. Rebuilding our respect for time to create, time to accomplish, time to build and/or discover comradeship (or even love)—might it not be a valuable public as well as personal asset in our new conditions of life? Do we really *want* fast love?

For life in the fast track doesn't call for much emotional investment beyond personal ambition, aggression, and anxiety. It probably discourages responsive, developed feelings for others. In the first place, there isn't time. In the second, how do you know your feelings will be reciprocated or even understood? You haven't really got acquainted with these people you have taken up with. And in addition, the expectation of changes in these relationships, as one or both of you go in another direction, inhibits deep attachments. So why take the risk of forming any? Losing them will bring only pain. It seems better not to care too much; then one won't suffer much. Of course that cuts down on the range of enjoyment too, but as the old proverb says, it's better to be safe than sorry.

Or is it? In times of change, are we really better off trying to adapt to the unexpected and the threatening if we don't have close comrades to work with or a sense of our competence in coping with the physical world or of the time it may take to get anything done? These are strong supports when we face a need to act in unforeseen circumstances. If we can't trust our maps and our rules don't seem to work, we are adrift in the undefined, problematic space between social and mental structures. All we can turn to for guidance is the "rock-bottom rationality" of common sense that Hofstadter cited, but that resource depends on shared experience. Such intuitive knowledge comes out of lived emotions, out of watching work being done and understanding that accomplishment may be slow, out of patience and of listening and of trying to judge, even in a changed world, what decisions are sensible or at least aren't fatal. We will certainly have to take risks in that future that shocks us so, but the risks may be less dangerous if we can see both old and new, if we resist seeing the present as totally distanced from the human past and ourselves as distanced from each other.

One process, at any rate, we have not got rid of: raising children. It's long and it's variegated and often surprising. Here's a brief report on the psychological effect on a parent:

Most of our friends, also now with children, found it overwhelming to have kids. Make no mistake about it. You have another person, a 24-hour responsibility. A child is not a stereo or wall-to-wall carpeting or a messy garage, the second car, or any other thing. You will have her for a very long time as your responsibility to train, argue with, nurture, love, share, be a kid with, to kid and tease, cook for. Think of having her (or your next one also) as a logical but also an irrational, creative act, for your own selfishness and total altruism.[8] *(Emphasis added)*

The only unusual thing about this vivid contemporary report is that it was written by the male parent, which indicates that opportunities to learn patience and process as part of child raising are open to both sexes. On the whole, however, our society still leaves the experience largely to women, for though the distance between fathers and children is decreasing, it's still there and still reflects patriarchal behavior roles. Another sort of distancing presents problems for both parents, in that teaching, sharing and learning the obligations, rewards and long-term responsibilities of emotional relations is a phenomenon pretty much isolated as an element of raising children. Coming to it in adult life, most of us bring little earlier training in intuitive involvements with changing, developing, and unpredictable living creatures. Having grown up in a market environment of fast acquisitions mediated by money, we have to learn from scratch the complicated ways of sustaining long-term but shifting personal connections.

At the same time that we learn, we are expected to teach both the value and the practice of morality and of social equity. But whereas in the past these important lessons would have been part of the teaching of skills, of making, doing, and handling living creatures, they now stand alone. Once upon a time they were embedded in and illustrated by lessons in the management of crops and animals, of hand-manufacturing and processing food and goods, and all of the other daily activities in which humans worked together. Implicitly one learned patience and how best to use time; one learned that good work stood up to use and shoddy work didn't. Our ancestors couldn't avoid paying attention to some matters we can ignore. Awareness of the hard but variable "thinginess" of things, and of the slow processes that went into training animals in the skills that were required of *them*, provided analogies for human-to-human relations. Nor was raising children split down the middle as it is today, when much education is conducted somewhere outside the family in a formal setting called a school, and is understood to deal with training for adult life in the impersonal world of work, while home is where one learns, quite separately, about morals, emotional values, and the obligations of humans to humans.

So raising children can serve as an example of the sort of area where old maps need to be modified but not thrown away. Right-wing conservatives don't want to hear about modification. The radicals of the 1960s concentrated on throwing old maps away because these charts, they felt, had been proven false according to the experience of life as felt by the young.

We can't really afford to follow either the right-wing or the radical position. We need courage to take risks and get rid of cobwebs and mildew, and we need as well the judgment that can give us some idea of how grave these risks may be: At times not taking risks may be more dangerous. And then we need the two virtues of the middle way: the commonsense ability to perceive new possibilities, and the patience to try them out and adjust them and try them again, and still wait to see how they work. Woman's place has always been better equipped to teach its citizens judgment and patience, and man's world to teach active courage. Melding the two together is part of a new, long process in which the human race can look both at separation and distancing, and at ways to grow together.

Chapter 10

TO DEAL WITH FUTURE SHOCK

by looking over one's shoulder at the past seems like an odd prescription unless thinking of time as a continuing process has become habitual. Our current passion for the instant, the new and the novel, works to the contrary. Consequently it narrows the span of the present and leaves us riding a knife-edge of immediate experience. There's a small class of Russian verbs that carry a particular suffix, *noot'*, which expresses instantaneity: To sneeze is a perfect example, *cheeknoot'*. At times it seems as if we were conducting our lives in exactly this atmosphere. If we want to stop sneezing, so to speak, to broaden the knife-edge we ride and convert it into a more comfortable saddle-shaped present, we will find that being aware of what happened yesterday helps us to understand what may happen tomorrow. Like the water in a wave, the molecules of data change, but the wave-as-process retains an identity even as it shifts its shape. It may crest, it may merge with others, but these transformations provide trend lines that are revealing of the forces at work within the fluid.

These transformations also reveal where trend lines break, where something below the surface affects the rhythms that we have learned to expect. Improper behavior, I've been saying, is often a precursor of major change. It indicates that something as yet unheeded demands attention and will, in time, force the redrawing of maps and the alteration of prescriptions. A sense of the past cannot only help us to register that something is happening; it can provide a scale to measure the size and the significance of the event.

Memory, moreover, is multidimensional. Looking back, we see not just one past event, but also the matrix out of which it grew and the forces that moved it from the present-of-the-time-that-is-now-past through stages that have not yet culminated in a present-that-is-already-becoming-past. If we can sort out some of the operations of the process that produced old definitions within an earlier frame of reference and shaped the directives that came out of them, we can get a handhold on the same process at work today.

These operations reflect directives from the map of politics and public affairs even though their reverberations are felt personally. Role and self interact, as prescriptions for proper behavior limit and direct individual actions, while the prescriptions themselves are the product of authority's instinctive drive to establish its legitimacy. Its success in this effort depends on there being agreement about the premises for action, on their general acceptability. Here is where history comes in. If the general population, whose job is to agree to the propositions of authority, has forgotten the past, those earlier occasions when premises were tested, it's easier for authority to gain a consensus. If past mistakes are forgotten, they don't have to be explained or justified. The credibility that the rest of us grant to the king or the president or the junta or the dictator permits him, her, or them to base orders merely on currently perceived data, the wave as it looks at the moment. Only the immediate data are important, the molecules of water churning about in today's pattern of activity. But when society accepts that view it is denying the existence of the wave, of the force that continually moves these molecules into changing patterns, patterns that may never repeat themselves exactly but will be influenced by those that appeared earlier and vary according to permanent laws of motion.

Using history, to reach for a more active comparison, is rather like learning a language. On the one hand, there's the vocabulary we struggle to memorize, which corresponds to the data to be used; on the other, there are rules of grammar and syntax and customary usage. But of course these factors aren't separate from each other: We never really get hold of the rules until we've acquired enough vocabulary-data to try them out in practice. Once we have grasped them, however, we can swing our vocabulary around as we want. We understand most of what other people are saying and we can reply reasonably well if not perfectly. Which means that we now have the power to influence actions among those who speak this language.

Certainly the data of language change and so do the rules of grammar. Equally the vocabulary of social usage and its goals and limits and prescriptions are open to alteration in many ways. At the moment, technological advance is producing the most sweeping shifts that humanity has ever lived through, not only in our relations with the physical world but with the world inside our heads.

By far the most potent new force that is influencing the process of definition today is television. It has changed the way that we perceive the world out there, and though we know that—have indeed been bombarded with analyses on the consequences for society, for the family, and for individual psychology—I don't believe that we have yet begun to appreciate the reach of its subliminal effects, of what we might call "the slow viruses." They not only get into our ways of seeing, they pervade the ways in which we weave our perceptions together into patterns that support and explain our thinking and our doing and both direct and hinder various kinds of relationships. The maps of meaning that we invent, or accept, are suddenly subject to change by unknown forces in ways that often take place below the level of conscious awareness. The effects of constant alteration, however, can be very disturbing since it's these maps we rely on for judging the world of actuality and events as well as the personalities of the people who live there, including ourselves.

To some degree, history can be directly useful in thinking about alterations in the possible ways in which we communicate with each other, for this kind of profound shift has happened before. The appearance of permanent records of some kind was clearly a factor that accompanied and facilitated the shift from a world of hunter-foragers, living in relatively small and somewhat nomadic groups, to the larger settled communities made possible by agriculture. With the use of written symbols custom, which is based on memory, gave way to systems of law. Ownership of land could be recorded, along with the taxes due to a central authority, which, in turn, would validate claims to ownership. Priestly castes appeared as guardians of sacred documents and holy objects. They became licensed interpreters and definers of the doctrines registered on tablets and scrolls. With the advent of the political state, social division by rank began to harden. History itself could now be born.

On the personal level, the capacity to list goods and record events surely had repercussions. Itineraries for travel by merchants were supplemented by maps of the night sky, useful in desert wastes and at sea. Recipes for medicines and magic spells as well as for meals not only registered technical knowledge but also established proper ways of doing things and, consequently, proper ways of thinking.

The consequences that followed the birth of writing can, of course, be imagined only in broad terms. Much more accessible are the results of the invention of printing. Literacy increased since more texts were available, and the multiplication of accurate, exact copies of manuscripts and documents, illustrations, maps and scientific diagrams promoted the spread of information. But less obvious results followed as well. A critical examination of knowledge by a much larger body of scholars was now possible. Both phenomena influenced activities in the world at some removal from the assiduous student. Trustworthy maps supplemented, or took the place of, ad hoc sailing directions from more or less literate sea captains and surely contributed to the ventures and discoveries of the age of exploration. Maps of the body, anatomical schemata that could be reproduced precisely, must have encouraged advances in the medical sciences. Did the proliferation of classical texts that could be compared and contrasted and consulted again and again establish the revival of learning in the fifteenth and sixteenth centuries as the Renaissance? Did the availability for comparison of scriptural texts, hitherto copied by hand with inevitable misreadings and variants, preserved for use only in ecclesiastical settings, strengthen the impulse to religious questioning of the same era and produce the Reformation? Earlier revivals of learning had sprung up under Charlemagne and in the twelfth century, and earlier heresies had flourished regionally, but they had disappeared as the centralized orthodoxy of Christian culture prevailed. At that time "burning the books" really could destroy knowledge that had been condemned. It was the invention of the printing press, declares Elizabeth Eisenstein, naming it "an agent of change,"[1] that gave new data and novel inventions permanent status and a wide-ranging presence which encouraged their inclusion in patterns of thought and thereby altered the patterns themselves.

Our ancestors, even the scholars and the activists who were fascinated by the potential uses of the printing press, did not foresee such a variety of consequences. And television, which has fallen on the entire globe like a whirlwind, is at least as hard to decipher. What is it doing to us, as citizens and as individuals? In spite of the avalanches of prognostication and discussion that greeted its birth and have accompanied its spread, we have not arrived at any satisfactory answer to that question. For one thing, the process is still going on. For another, television has not yet defined itself. Instead it has chosen to wear a mask of "entertainment," a matter to which I will return. Again, most evaluations of its impact concentrate on the content of the programs it shows and therefore, on the direct, purposive use of the medium. Its most important effects, however, are peripheral and complex. Critics and prophets have worried about these from the start but when the process was newborn, evaluating it and predicting its uses were hard.

Let me start with the last point. Television's baptismal ceremony was attended by a good godfather who came with a blessing, Marshall McLuhan, and a bad one who foresaw only evil, George Orwell. McLuhan envisaged a future in which instant communication across the world would gather humanity into a "global village." That doesn't seem to be happening. Looking at strangers, we see strangers. A view of starving peasants in famine-ridden Africa awakens pity but it is rather like the pity that morally aware middle-class folk in turn-of-the-century London felt for "the people of the abyss"; fear and revulsion are present too. We help these unfortunates not because they are like us, but in the hope that a bit of sacrifice will do something to prevent our ever becoming like them. Let their otherness be distant! Again, shots of the Vietnam war were disturbing enough to divide the country politically; but the effect was due less to fellow feeling for the victims of violence among the watching audience than to self-centered feelings aroused there. Watchers were shaken by moral repugnance for the role of American combat troops or, on the other hand, by shame at the ineffectiveness of our military might in the face of a technologically backward enemy. It was our own failings Americans worried about far more than the disasters that had fallen on a segment of the global village. We saw difference, not likeness.

Orwell's vision set down in 1948 of the police state of *1984* has not been realized either. Television, he imagined, could be used not only for propaganda but also for intimate surveillance of an entire populace. Now individual surveillance is quite possible. A recent note in *Scientific American*[2] reports on "the swift advance of communication technology [which] has outpaced the laws protecting individual privacy." Devices are available to keep track of movements and conversation behind locked doors, which sensitive microphones can pick up and deliver to computers that can then edit them for relevant references. Cameras that work in the dark, monitoring of telephones and electronic mail, and many other surveillance techniques can now be focused on suspects.

But which suspects? Who decides who will be subjected to these extensive, and expensive, measures? And who will evaluate the data thus collected? No state has enough personnel to check out videotapes and recordings of data covering any considerable percentage of the population, and certainly none has enough to supply monitors whose political sophistication can be trusted. Indeed grave doubts have been raised about the consequences of granting security clearances to as many Americans as now hold them. The increase in recent espionage-for-money, it is suggested, is a direct result of unwarranted and unnecessary secrecy. Invent an area that is labeled "secret" but which requires a lot of policing and you have invented opportunities for commercial disloyalty. The label itself defines the contents as valuable. "Who polices the police?" has been a vital question for millennia, and it won't ever be solved by technology, no matter how advanced. In itself, widespread surveillance is evidence that authority doubts the persuasiveness of its definition; that it fears for its own legitimacy. Such fears are catching.

Orwell's vision of television as an instrument of universal surveillance was, I think, influenced by the historical circumstances of the late 1940s when the medium was brand-new and when Hitler's Germany and Stalin's Russia were recent or continuing facts of existence: historical data, ripe for assessment. Orwell seized on it—and got it wrong. But was it history, or was it his imaginative estimate of the new technology that misled him? The latter, it seems to me. For in fact actual police states don't behave like the regime of Big Brother, but that was less easy to see then than now.

The impact of new inventions is most difficult to judge when they *are* new and colored by what we impute to them; *1984* probably owes as much to creative paranoia as it does to history.

Police states forty years later, at any rate, still prefer old methods. In 1985 South Africa, well on its way to deserving the label, turned its back on television and banned reporters and reportage as being unpredictable and dangerous. Dictatorships certainly watch identified suspects and infiltrate dubious organizations. They arrest suspect individuals on the basis of rumor and hearsay as much as on warranted evidence, lock them up, torture them, exile them, or simply contrive that they disappear—from the little princes in the Tower during the reign of Richard III of England to the vanished thousands of young and old during the reign of the junta in Argentina. All of these techniques for controlling or destroying opposition involve human judgment: Which intimates of suspects can be subverted? How much can one rely on what they say? What kind of blackmail will work? Electronic surveillance can extend the range where such questions can be asked but it doesn't provide answers. Indeed an overload of information is apt to jam the circuits.

The social and political effects of television are very great, but they are part of a much larger and more subtle whole. To make a start on understanding the whole—and we can't do much more than make a start even now—we want to look not at the medium itself but at the relationships that have developed between it and its audience. Needless to say, some of its effects have been analyzed nearly to death and subjected to countless attacks, many of them well-founded. Television contributes to the growth of illiteracy by offering a vivid alternative to reading, especially for those whose first language was not that of the schools. It produces shortened attention spans and so it intensifies contemporary tendencies to speed things up and to make thinking usefully about the past more difficult. The immediate present, in fact, is always the scene of action. Past action is simply presented as a rerun of a former present. It is not subjected to emotional or intellectual judgment because no way has yet been devised to show it as different: There are no tenses in this language.

On the stage, contrariwise, actors who are there in the flesh and thus immediately present to the audience know how to shift the focus of meaning in many ways; or rather the whole ensemble, from playwright to lighting director, knows how. Monologues directed to the audience have been accepted as spoken thoughts at least since the time of Shakespeare. Shifting the lighting reflects moods, and changes in acting tone emphasize some speeches and deny the value of others implicitly. For various reasons, some of which we'll discuss, there has been more room in films to experiment with the presentation of experience, and a symbolic language of flashbacks, of blurred effects, of swift cuts between sequences, and so on has begun to develop. The use of innovative techniques has characterized filmmaking from its earliest days, whether they are subtle and nuanced or depend on the spectacular "special effects" so popular today. Both approaches respond to the urge toward freshness that lies at the core of creativity, though the latter usually relies too heavily on mechanics. Still, the impulse to experiment in any form is a sign of health.

In the case of television, the cost of mechanical marvels inhibits experimentation while the chosen label of "entertainment" hinders the serious presentation of complex emotional states, which might produce disturbing responses or simple confusion. Instead a kind of jolting immediacy is employed in an effort to keep us riveted to the screen. A show of violence is the method most frequently used, but another effective attention-getter is the presentation of material objects that awaken urgent emotions of envy and greed. These symbols of high status demonstrated by ostentatious wealth show up as dramatic backgrounds to the sagas of television's dynasties of aristo-plutocrats, but they come closer to the audience in the game shows that make them seem tantalizingly available with minimal effort. The lucky people who have gained access to these lotteries don't look very different from you and me!

Since material objects can never, by their nature, be fully satisfying for very long (unless they are transmuted into symbols standing for some transcendental value), such covetousness increases frustration and dissatisfaction, emotions that are alienating in the extreme. Like speeded-up time, they reduce the value of actual winning, actual possession, actual feelings of pleasure, which have been felt as a just reward and remain in memory to justify what has been gained. On the television screen we are continually being shown a never-never-land that we can't touch. Even the winners of new microwave ovens and matched sets of luggage have to take them away from their glamorous settings and the applauding studio audiences and install them in everyday space. One wonders how much glamour vanishes in the move. This kind of double vision diminishes what we have in favor of what we don't have. Even when we get what we long for, the aura of desire that functions as propaganda for "the good life" ends when the prize falls into our hands. Aside from the moral question of whether we really value what we haven't worked for—and something of the Protestant ethic still lingers in our society—winners are open to psychological doubts about whether they really deserve these goodies. For the audience, of course, these bits of the good life flash by so fast that it's hard to feel them as real. There is no hard concrete thinginess to these things.

More important, however, are the limits placed on the possible aims of any medium that accepts external boundaries to its treatment of material. Within its limits it offers positive rewards. It would hardly attract the huge audiences it enjoys if it didn't deliver pleasure and fill gaps in the existence of its viewers that have been growing wider with the loss of settled life in a small, familiar community, where human nature, good or bad, can be known intimately. Television supplies a feasible replica of the gossip that used to be an arresting part of everyday life. Lonely old ladies don't have to snoop out their windows anymore, they can turn on the afternoon soap operas, and what they see is a lot more exciting than most of what their neighbors are doing. Moreover it isn't as puzzling. Superficially the motivation for action on the small screen is supplied, though its rationale and plausibility are painfully deficient if one starts to think about them. The need for suspense truncates realistic development of action, but it arises from a necessity to keep us looking and guessing; narrative logic is the first victim in any variety of melodrama. Still, life itself is surprising, noisy, and at times highly colored and swiftly moving. Soap opera plots heighten what is sometimes there, in daily life, and ignore the weeks of boredom that intervene between the occasional crises. In doing so, however, they weaken or suppress any sense of duration, of passing time. But, on the positive side, we can see that television offers widened experience to its viewers, companionship to the lonely, amusement to the unhappy, and a general, if surface, flow of information about the world and the people in it. It's a grayed-down version of McLuhan's vision of integration through communication.

Two kinds of programs claim to be more than, or at least different from, contrived entertainment: news broadcasts and sports events. Since the latter are inherently entertaining, their nature is the least changed of all by television presentation. It isn't necessary to process them to any great extent, simply to make visible what is going on; though even here, instant replay is producing questions about the credibility of umpires' decisions and may end by changing the actual events in some fashion. These programs, however, don't need much heightening since an enthusiastic, knowledgeable audience is eager to watch and ready to criticize what it sees in a tolerably expert way. Sport as an aesthetic experience is so much part of American life that producers play around with its presentation at their peril. But sports contests are themselves predictable. They are bound by known rules that must be observed (and instant replay simply makes the matter of enforcing the rules more interesting) whatever the outcome of any particular contest may be.

News programs stand on middle ground between entertainment and actual events in situations that aren't bound by any rules of the game but must be made comprehensible to the audience. Tradition tells newscasters that a primary duty is to tell the truth. They would like to. But whose truth? The size of the audience, in itself, forces a least-common-denominator approach. Complicated truth takes time to tell, is debatable, and often in flux. And then there are ideologies to be considered. How much weight can their adherents swing with sponsors? Print media can deal with this problem by addressing fairly small but identifiable audiences, but television is too pricey for such an approach and leaves it to radio. The producers of network news programs are always stuck with a narrow range of material that all the networks agree to be important, vivid, and readily comprehensible: suitable, that is, for keeping people looking at their sets with some interest between commercials. As a result, the personality of the news team, most especially the anchor, assumes enormous significance. "What's happening" is shown through a lens that is affected by the need to entertain and by the personal plausibility of the presenter. At any time, the current public status of women and minority members can be estimated by their frequency as newscasters.

But of course sports and news don't make up the bulk of programming on television. How are we to define the rest of it: label it, assign it to appropriate maps, give it importance, and judge the prescriptions that it puts forward, the last being an activity it doesn't much like to admit? Generally, discussions of the effects of television falter in one of two ways. Either they approach the content of the programs directly, prepared to judge them on grounds of morality or educational value, or they regard them as harmless, as the entertainment they claim to be, which passes time without leaving any significant mark on the mind or the character of the viewer.

Both approaches ask the wrong kinds of questions. It's more productive, I believe, to consider the programs and the responses they evoke in terms of aesthetic considerations. The problem begins with the label. "Entertainment" as used in this connection means not only an aspiration to please as many viewers as possible but also to displease as few. The shadow of the sponsor's reaction to negative responses lies across the capacity of television to risk showing new and possibly dangerous material; in this it resembles the censorship of foreign news reporting by the South African government. Indeed, it's even more explicit and effective: "Don't even try to show what's problematic," it says.

That's hardly news. We've all read or heard stories about the instinct to copy successful formulas that is part of a great deal of programming. One can't really question that reaction. These people are paid to increase sales by advertisers. Of course they don't want to irritate potential buyers! There's nothing surprising or immoral about such a desire. The difficulties that arise aren't moral; they are precisely aesthetic. They prevent television from moving past the goal of entertainment toward involvement with serious art.

Serious art doesn't mind beginning in entertainment. It has often done just that. Even in modern times when folk-style has been separated from fine arts (at least by the "academy") practitioners of the latter have turned to the former for refreshment and even for new ways of seeing: Think of all those nineteenth-century composers working with traditional melodies in collaborations that enriched both sides; go play the "Trout Quintet." Think of the continuing pressure of primitive art on studio art, of high comedy and classic farce. No student of drama should neglect the pace of Feydeau's ridiculous contrivances; they have something to say about revelation scenes from Oedipus on. European and American artists of the last century have turned to Oriental,

African, and Native American cultures for inspiration, as our own folk culture has been increasingly influenced by technology. Finally the need to communicate with everyday actuality has begun to bring the human significance of life in a technological culture into serious art. But time for exploration and for realization of the unprecedented destruction of old links and the discovery and creation of new ones is required. Television's insistence on novelty and speeded-up responses impedes its approach to seriousness here, as in other areas.

Serious art, to be didactic, can use almost any sort of material as its base. What it can't do is to work toward two goals that are incompatible. But what psychological process can do that? The classic result is neurotic stasis and frustration. Double-mindedness that is not allowed to mingle its purposes is more limiting, more debilitating to creativity, than are rules that tell the artist to work within the limits of strict form. In fact poetry has thrived on restrictive form: Japanese haiku provide an extraordinary example of concentrated energy within a tiny syllabic expanse. Television's difficulties arise less from the limits placed on what it can treat than on demands that it do two things at once: entertain people, and refrain from disturbing them.

For human beings cannot live in a constant condition of trivial pursuit, no matter how delightful periods of relaxed foolishness can be. We need serious art; most simply we need it in order to deepen our experience and to validate and make accessible human emotions and our necessary wrestling with the human condition. None of us is going to escape love or tragedy or rage or running into blank walls that assure us we can't have what we want, nor terror and hate and deprivation. These dooms, or exaltations, are what art deals with. Its presence in our lives increases the range of existence in which we can walk without fear of the unknown, in conditions of absolute loneliness, caught in that terrible space between our maps where (it seems) no one else has ever had to dwell. But of course other people have been there, and writers and painters and musicians and sculptors have wrestled with the experience, sometimes for sheer survival but always in order to report on extreme conditions, on life at the edge. Out of their struggles comes the most intense expression of the significance of our culture.

What exists of this expression today is not central to our lives, and for many reasons besides television, which is a phenomenon that I am trying to analyze, not to attack. But the time-filling distraction that television offers does habituate us to the absence of the old, valuable, and hitherto fairly universal connection with serious art. We look for transcendence in other places, by other means. But the most usual means, drugs and sex, are individual and personal.

Art connects the individual to wider truths and to the myths that grow out of common experience. In the past our own society, with its western European roots, which are still quite central to our ways of seeing and thinking in spite of an inpouring of material from other cultures, created its own versions of art centered around philosophic and religious questions, from which developed emotional styles that moved into the secular world. But the matters discussed by art have continued to be serious: fundamental explorations of meaning and human dignity, of rites and ceremonies that express continuing concerns, of dance and music that seek to join private emotion with the presentation of shared truths. If folk-style differs in form, that is because it centers in different material: tales and song and dance and competitive games that are tied to the work cycle of the year. But the dailiness of work does not reject religious ritual; nor does ceremony turn its back on the necessity and the meaning of labor. Together both forms of art *place* participants in time and space and existence. They provide points and patterns on maps and prescribe appropriate ways for understanding and expressing the emotions called up by common experience. The power to define is at work here, in its deepest function, to structure the chaos of life.

Since for many of us alive today, chaos is all too familiar, I think there should be few surprises in the revivalist fundamentalism that has had such a swift rebirth in the last couple of decades. It speaks of a search for expository, explanatory myths to guide our faltering footsteps by calling on known ceremonies and celebrations. The problems that go with revivalism are, unfortunately, quite as evident, for fear of chaos breeds intolerance and a refusal to consider the causes of chaos. Fundamentalism is one answer to the hovering problems of contemporary life, but not a relevant one, which is true of a lot of answers to pressing needs, after all.

The fact that fundamentalist religious services are widely present on television, services that are fully aware of the core definition of the medium as entertainment, demonstrates its usefulness as an answer machine. So far, its fear of risk taking means that it can only copy, repeat, exploit, and to an extent misuse the most accepted and familiar myths of our culture. The whole context of triviality makes serious talk on serious subjects seem out of place, while the value of celebrity-personality concentrates attention on the sermonizer, not the sermon. The answers that religion is able to convey via television simply don't, or can't, speak deeply to the dangers of the processes loose in our time.

We shouldn't ignore the price exacted by the enforced choice of superficiality made by this powerful medium, which is thus rendered incapable of its full use. Its watered-down presence is always with us, gossipy, entertaining, distracting, showing us people who catch our attention and present themselves as if they were living in real space, the world out there. The refusal of television to develop its extraordinary new techniques for serious purposes, together with the replacement of aesthetic experiment by doublethink and commercial exploitation, produces something more than failure. It produces distortion and falsity, there's no way around it.

I daresay that television does not mean to do that. It

sincerely wants to live up to its label of simple, satisfying entertainment. But human beings looking at other human beings in dramatic action for hours on end are going to take this entertainment seriously. These people on the screen look like real-life characters we meet in the flesh. They may not exactly act like them but they approach expected "normal" behavior closely enough for us to accept them as representations of the way things are. Look long enough and habituation will begin to persuade you that the world does work this way: speeded-up, heightened, suspenseful, surprising, and therefore very hard to predict. Because trivial entertainment does not dare involve us in deeper and disturbing emotions, it is sentenced to keep our attention by keeping us guessing.

It's easy to find unpredictability plausible. Our world is big and strange, we constantly mingle with people we know nothing about, and settled patterns of behavior, understandable and familiar, aren't constants in our lives as they were for our peasant ancestors growing up in village communities. Our uncertainties give weight to the messages from the medium that tell us life is random all around, very apt to get out of control.

That kind of statement is politically powerful. "You don't know what's going to happen next," says the action on the tube, and it's a prescription for observant passivity. From time to time I do a tour of duty looking at afternoon soaps and evening miniseries and melodramas, and the steady assertion that comes through is that these people are like us in that they have terrible problems. Their problems are solved (when they are, otherwise the characters tend to vanish) by chance and random luck. The goddess of fortune is a capricious lady, and those who try to solve their own problems are apt to run into trouble, for how can they oppose her whims? No one really knows what is going to happen next and if you think you do, Fortune will be particularly happy to prove you wrong. No newcomer to the scenes of these dramas is completely trustworthy, though some people are almost absolutely untrustworthy; just the same, they might surprise you one day and do you a favor in order, perhaps, to confuse you. No love is certain; let a wedding date be set and you can all but count on a hitch in the festivities. Even death can't be certified. The corpse is apt to turn up in good health in some future segment, having had an attack of amnesia or found it necessary to flee the police, or been lost in the woods after a "fatal" plane crash. Mistaken identity is a constant reminder of existential uncertainty. Is a long-lost sister what she claims to be, or a clever imposter? Any stranger may harbor some sinister purpose. Welcome a cousin to your lovely home and you're likely to discover that she intends to kidnap your child, seduce your spouse, or reveal at an awkward moment that your first husband was a spy for the KGB and you are suspected of harboring his papers (I made up that last bit myself, but it may well have been used without my knowing it). If you want to know what happens next, tune in tomorrow! It's no good your trying to use your wits or your judgment to work out the consequences of what you've been watching.

Is nothing certain, then? No, there is one perennial character who breaks the pattern of randomness: the hero. Strong, virile, upstanding, stop-at-nothing heroes can change the world—violently, of course. That message is more conscious than is the pervasive warning of randomness and unpredictability that is simply a by-product of the need to keep people looking. Heroes are solitary, individual, often loners, often justified in their violence because it is definable as revenge for injustice. They act for us against the Establishment world; and that too suggests the passivity of the viewing audience. For like the trickster-heroes of old myth, they ask, "Are you strong enough to take the risks that we accept? If not, stay home. Don't try to act for yourselves." The political effect of that repeated statement is, as it always has been, to keep members of the governed majority from joining together and acting for themselves. If action is associated with the lone hero and his wild bravado, then other sorts of action are made unattractive. "Don't try to help yourself," say such tales. "Have a hero instead."

The popularity of the shows that feature these heroes hints at what television might do if it was willing to be serious across the board, for it *is* serious in these presentations. The old myths of individual daring and courage are alive and infinitely transferable to the screen in up-to-the-minute terms. Here is one genre of programming where strong emotions can be expressed and, conversely, where talent and money are free to explore an important human concern, the anatomy of risk taking. These programs rivet audiences because they speak authoritatively of a known world where violence is entirely plausible. Television can for once forget its servitude to moral shibboleths. Its reflections on violence as a normal part of urban existence, which can be met unquestioningly by counterviolence, are dangerous but credible. This world we see is a world we know, heightened and made immediate, but not falsified. We do, alas, need heroes. The question is what kind.

Let me sum up these efforts at defining television by stating a simple, taken-for-granted conclusion: People looking at television are strongly affected by what they see. The medium may try to wash its hands of influencing its viewers in disturbing ways and repeat that its sole purpose is entertainment, but it's not a convincing proposition: "We don't pretend that it's true," say the programmers. "It's not our fault if they believe it."

But all through human history, people have looked at other people and taken what they see happening as representing reality: proper behavior, in the sense that human beings do act that way. They have thereupon drawn conclusions from this behavior that are generalized into conceptions of causality and process and the predictability of events. Drama, ceremony, and serious art of all kinds don't dispute those conclusions. They take what we see and what we feel and our judgments on the events of our lives and go in search of the structures that lie therein. They are looking for meanings, and of course they can go wrong. But their purpose is to refine reality into truth that is more intense and more coherent than the data of everyday existence. They don't want to falsify but to eliminate what is irrelevant to that truth.

When television declares that it is merely entertainment, it's shifting priorities. Amusing irrelevancy comes first, truth is much too solemn and out of place to be of concern, and plausibility is there to be stretched to the limit. Television neither presents boring old everyday life with all its loose ends, nor intensifies or purifies these oddments of data in order to reveal the shape of the wave. It nudges truth only in its presentation of violent heroes and reality only when, as in sports and news, there are rules that have to be honored.

Television, in short, is programmed.

Well now! Don't we all know that? Yes, oh yes, we do; that's the label displayed in the listings for the sequences of events we look at. But do we grant this simple, familiar statement all the importance it should have? Do we really differentiate between what happens out there in the street or in the office or at home, and what is presented to us on the screen as happening there? Do we? It is only on the rarest occasions that what we are shown by television has not been processed by a human brain (more likely several human brains) other than our own. What we see is selected. Are we always conscious of what that means or do we naturally, humanly, suppose that what we see and experience *is* experience, all more or less of the same kind?

Take violence that is present in so many programs that it is an expected part of the mix. Every now and then something violent really happens, right there where we expect unreal violence, something unannounced and actual. For me the memorable event was the moment when Jack Ruby shot Lee Harvey Oswald before my eyes. It was unbelievable, shocking in the truest sense. Here was a man dying, *it was real*, it was going on at that very moment, no "programming" about it. I daresay the assassination of John Kennedy carried the same quality of being beyond belief but I was not watching the tube at that moment. Oswald's death remained for me different, beyond all the reruns of the assassination itself, painful as it was to watch those. Even the launch of the Challenger did not quite match Oswald's—execution? murder? For although we knew by sight the human beings aboard and understood what must be happening to them as flames engulfed the shuttle, we didn't see their deaths with our own eyes. I don't know whether we should be grateful for that or not; the act of bearing witness is an important one. But in any case, those deaths took place out of sight. They were distanced from the viewers.

Vietnam and its horrors were different in a different way. We saw the violence all right, but it had a more ambiguous feel to it. The same thing is true of recent terror in Lebanon and South Africa. It's not simply that we have seen so much over the years; it's that what we are shown is put into a setting. It is presented, and we are somehow prepared. Someone has cut the footage and edited it, someone speaks a voice-over description. I wonder sometimes whether something as clearly unprogrammed as the moments when Ruby's gun swung up, Oswald's face puckered, and his hands clutched at his belly would still be unmistakably different. I'm not sure. In any case, our perception of the difference would only occur, I think, in as extreme a case as that one, where immediate reality was guaranteed. Where we knew that the only editor was fate.

Neither news programs nor sports events, then, are real exceptions to the fact that television is generally programmed. The editing of news is clearly necessary in order to present the important core events; but someone is deciding what these important events are. Meaning is given to them before we watchers have a chance to look for ourselves, and it alters what we see.

Programming works a little differently for sports events, limited by their own rules. Even when some improper behavior occurs, it's predictable *in kind*. McEnroe is going to lose his temper at a linesman. Some furious pitcher or hitter or runner is going to charge the baseball umpire who has called him out. The manager is going to tumble out of the dugout swearing and sputtering and join the fray, and we are about to be given a chance to see, once more, the imperial swing of the arm that sends someone off the field. What is happening is a ritual, applied to a temporal event. The World Series of 1985 and 1986 provided telling examples of drama, different enough in emotional tone to illustrate the range of theatrics that sports events can supply. In 1985 when St. Louis seemed assured of victory, Fate herself took a hand in the game: A disputed call by the first-base umpire altered the climate of success that had made the Cardinals favorites as if a north wind had swept down from the Arctic. In the last game their misfortunes provided viewers with an exhaustive demonstration of the meaning of "debacle." No one watching would ever need to ask what the word meant.

The 1986 Series was even more unpredictable. Guessing the winner became an exercise in assessing indeterminancy. But the kind of contest that was taking place was clear. 1985 could be labeled as a reversal of probability. 1986 proclaimed itself to be a classic tight race, heightened by luck, shifted one way by human error and back again by phenomenal human exploits. 1985 recalled the folk tales where a malign magician intervenes. 1986 spelled out the essential nature of suspense on the human scale.

In each Series, that is, the specific outcome was unpredictable, but the style of the performance was identifiable. We knew where we were in terms of the aesthetics of sports and so the climax of winning, or losing, was intensified. Its meaning was foreshadowed and was therefore emotionally satisfying.

In fact, we were looking at drama, perfectly done in the proper aesthetic vein; and in drama, climax and denouement shape the map and make it predictable. It would take a couple of masked men with machine guns, mowing down the whole defensive backfield of one of the Rose Bowl contenders, to break the expected pattern convincingly. The excitement in sports events is channeled, directed, and heightened artistically by the rules of what's aesthetically permissible and pertinent to this form of art. Because sports are subject to such rules, they are the shows that are most satisfying to watch and approach excellence most closely.

But for the great bulk of programming, the rules aren't set and known to all. Come back to the old ladies who no longer snoop out the window at the neighbors' carryings-on because they can look at *General Hospital* instead. The important difference is this: In life the deck hasn't been stacked, which is of course likely to make for some very dull games. On the tube, the sequence of happenings is not happening by itself. It has been processed.

And, once again, it has been processed for a purpose that is inattentive to actual causes and real processes of events and chooses to use speeded-up artifice instead. The randomness of soap-opera plots substitutes melodramatic fabrications for causal sequences as we experience them in life. These sequences are slow moving, hard to recognize, and often unwelcome, and so are apt to run counter to television's aim to entertain. Serious art, however, is one of the human enterprises charged with searching out, by aesthetic means, the messages, changing or repetitive, somber or joyful, that reality supplies for our guidance. It can't stop the flow of events or switch them about or toss in an amusing scene because someone tells it to do so. It may do all those things, but only as experiments, conducted because they may (or may not) reveal the inner sense of the story or the music or the picture. In the end the work stops when the structured material says, "That's complete. Quit." But television programs have to work within limits and according to directives that are not pertinent to the process of creation.

And that means that they are false. Not on purpose, but by the iron law of making art, for nothing that can't take risks can approximate truth. Taking risks, of course, is no guarantee that a great and truthful work will emerge, but being unable to take them, forbidden to take them, is a guarantee that such a work can't be produced.

So when viewers look at events on the screen and casually, naturally, tuck them away in memory as "experience," they are making an easy but dangerous mistake. Experience of processed life is not equivalent to remembered actuality. It can't be used as a trustworthy base for conclusions about what's likely or improbable in the world off the screen. All our lives we've been observing and interacting and judging and responding to people; now before us there are creatures who look just like the real people we know (well, perhaps not the hair). True, we can't interact with them, but that's true too of the characters we meet in books or dreams, look at in pictures, or hear about in history classes. If their stories or their personae interest us, we can respond internally to these figures without confusing them with those we meet in real life.

But now we have a whole pack of observations of people who seem real but are in fact skewed away from actuality. The material of experience that we have always counted on to form judgments about the world is contaminated by— toxic waste? In the past the experience we used as a way for choosing proper, useful behavior came out of things that had really happened to us or had been told or shown to us as experience that matched the premises of the world we lived in. And now that is not true anymore.

What does that mean for children especially, to whom all experience, real or made up, is unfamiliar territory that must be learned? How do they sort it out? Or do they?

Chapter 11

TELEVISION'S CHOSEN IDENTITY

as our preeminent entertainer doesn't interfere with its preeminence as an instrument for defining the contemporary world; the two functions work together. The medium's structural need to program, sequence, and connect the chaos of reality provides viewers with a sense of security. We may not know just what is going on, but someone has constructed what we see, and done so in terms designed to be comprehensible. The people we meet belong to categories we recognize, and identify themselves consistently if simplistically. They may be scoundrels or deceivers but their tricks are familiar from the tradition of melodrama and when we can place them there, their chicaneries don't confront us with the unsettling dilemmas we find, and fear, in real life. Programs are arranged, while life happens.

Unscheduled disasters can't be excluded from action on the screen, of course. Terrorist bombings and glimpses of hostages in the hands of their captors flash before our eyes like snapshots from nightmare. They remain puzzling, and television, being quite aware that they cannot be programmed, or examined seriously in any acceptable time-scheme, simply shows what it can: dispatches from chaos. News commentary is most persuasive when it's most obvious. The messages we get tend to tell us that America is under attack from evil people whose behavior is vengeful but unmotivated by rational purposes. We witness a series of what appear as unrelated shocks that distance us emotionally from their perpetrators. The only coping behavior that's presented as possible is some kind of activist policy, which will have to be undertaken by experts who resemble those parental giants who protected us from dangers and nastiness in our childhood. Current declines in the audience for news programs emphasize that it isn't bad news we want when we turn on the television set.

And most of the time we don't get it. Television won't force us to look at what doesn't please us. It seems an obedient servant, ingratiating, accommodating, with no intention of dictating ideas or prescribing behavior. Its first act is to give us a choice of programs. If we look at the disasters that the news reports, it's by our own decision. We could perfectly well shift the channel to something pleasanter and enjoy a scenario designed to distract us from anxiety, not to awaken it. A little experience teaches us that the general run of programs are similar in range and in the material they present: After all, they must manage to be popular enough to survive and therefore must appeal to the wide, if shallow, consensus of interesting relationships, admired figures, and desired ends that's current at any time. The consensus can shift quickly, in the way that fashions in dress do, as long as the changes are minor, but it finds it hard to accept eccentricity. At most any eccentric character we see plays a fairly familiar role and stays within it. American society doesn't tolerate eccentricity that is freewheeling and unexpected; oddities who can't be placed are labeled "abnormal," which is not a category one wishes to enter. Young people, especially, who are trying to learn their way around the society they were born into, don't enjoy the name. They certainly seize on roles that diverge from those regarded as proper by adults, but these roles have their own characteristics that are endorsed and maintained by peer pressure.

Television, the ubiquitous and amusing communicator, is particularly attractive to the young because its variety of programs does seem to offer a choice and, therefore, the appearance of control over what one selects to look at. Even more compelling for their elders is the relief from isolation that turning on the switch provides. "The illusion of companionship sits waiting in the television set," writes Louise Bernikow in her recent study of contemporary loneliness, *Alone in America.* We need that illusion so badly, she adds, that "we keep our televisions on more than we watch them—an average of seven hours a day. For background. For company."[1] The daily excitements of family events in the lives of our imaginary friends, the gossip about the extraordinary doings of the rich and famous, are as absorbing as they are illogical. In fact their lack of logic is amusing because it's amazing; the very rich are indeed different from you and me. At the same time, these astonishing events give rise to recognizable emotions. We'd feel the same way as these characters do if a family feud threatened to knock us out of the line of inheritance, or if a prodigal brother returned and declared that our intended bride was really waiting for him. And so we accept the fundamental grounds underlying the coloratura antics of the programs.

Indeed the basic conditions of life on which television builds its dramas are not only shared with us viewers; they are far older than either television or us. Any definitions and prescriptions for behavior that television supplies grow out of generations of human experience and reflect long-lived social problems. The loneliness that Bernikow speaks of has haunted Western society for generations, for the breakdown of close communities and lives lived face-to-face is part of the long process of urbanization and industrialization. Emile Durkheim, studying possible causes for a growth in Europe's suicide rate back in the 1890s, attributed many of these deaths to "anomie," to a growing loss of rewarding personal connections between society and the individual, a loss that diminishes the felt value of one's identity.

It's natural enough that a popular medium will use the underlying emotional strains in everyday life as a base for its productions. They contribute an unconscious plausibility to tales whose immediate content is ready to sacrifice credibility for arresting dramatic touches. Certainly the episodes that caution the audience against trusting those who present themselves as friends jibe with the all but universal experience of living among strangers. A world of strangers also emphasizes the value of continuity, of a process that may be full of surprises, but that carries us along from one surprise to the next. The plots and counterplots shown on the tube, extraordinary in themselves, still make use of definitions that their authors believe to be pertinent to ordinary lives. Mapped and sequenced, they are easier to read than are the surprises we get from the ups and downs of metropolitan chaos or from the people we are apt to meet there, who tend to be as confused as we are. So the comfort of illusory companionship via the tube is increased by finding solutions to problems there. They too may be illusory, but at least they suggest that solutions of some kind do exist, that rules for behavior are possible.

Another kind of widespread uneasiness that television responds to is the flattening out of life that has followed the disappearance of the regular celebrations and festivals that once marked turning points of the year, both religious and work-related. Harvest festivals and saint's days of fast or feast lit up the lives of our ancestors and marked each individual's passage through life as a person. Identity depends on memory. It is given us, and is confirmed, by recurrence, by annual holidays, and by partaking in rites of passage that are social in purpose but also identify each of us as a member of a known group of human beings, a community. Christenings, bar mitzvahs, graduations, marriages, here a personal existence crosses and joins a larger world. And if there are special family customs that mark these holidays, if the Christmas gifts are always distributed at one particular time and followed by a traditional meal; if the Passover seder is held in the same family home with the passage of time both illustrated and tamed through the changed identity of the child who asks the ritual questions, as one youngest succeeds another; if there are recurring picnics and fireworks viewings and attendance at fairs—all of them become eloquent reminders of individual experience which is placed within a sustaining community. But as families have been moving apart or have been broken through divorce, as towns have been deserted by the departure of city-bound young people, or neighborhoods have been transformed by gentrification, these temporal patterns have dimmed along with other maps and left us prey not only to loneliness but to "anomie." We are precisely more anonymous than were our ancestors.

Television, then, starts in the world as we know it through our feelings. It refuses to confront a good many painful matters; it turns away from presenting our difficulties in depth because as entertainment it must reject seriousness, controversy, and dispute; but—like all entertainment—it must show us scenes and characters we can recognize. It must speak in a language of drama that we know, by means of events that we can follow emotionally. It uses myths and updates legends, but they of course are familiar too. By its insistent dedication to superficial resolutions of the dilemmas it presents, it distorts and falsifies reality, but it nevertheless refers to real problems, widespread anxieties, and common distress. And thus it maintains the plausibility of shared feelings that gives it its power as a definer.

Almost instinctively, then, it moves to fill gaps in experience left by the loss of customs and holiday rituals that marked the year. It gives us scenes of ancient celebrations attuned to our current expectations. We see Christmas in Bethlehem and Christmas in Rockefeller Center when the tree is lit, the Macy's parade on Thanksgiving, and such invented annual spectacles as The Miss America pageant and the Oscar awards. Indeed these happenings were *not* invented by television, simply taken over and made universally visible. Like the climactic finale of the football season with its procession of bowl games, these events are both staged and actual, but the staging, which is television's work, establishes their importance. Here is a new calendar to place us in the year. It's not sacred, of course, but the coverage and the reportage of detail is so fervent that feelings are invited to run high, while the intimacy of our view increases the immediacy of what we're looking at. Indeed it's likely that television would rather stage celebrations that were already in being than to invent its own. Their previous history endorses their importance, which, in turn, is heightened by the attention focused on them by television-the-definer.

But what exactly are these celebrations significant of? What do they symbolize? Television can't or won't say. Deep explanations of meaning are out of place in a medium that prefers Disneyland to reality. Analyzing itself and its motives is distasteful, it contradicts the image and the self-image of a medium that, like Noël Coward, claims only "a talent to amuse." We may wonder whether that's all we ask of the wonderful machine that chats away for seven hours a day, but there's no use in asking television what its purpose is. Not that it will refuse to answer. It will reply at once: Its purpose is to make money. Isn't that important enough? Isn't that a good American aim?

There's a lot to be said for that position. Our society is indeed money-oriented and cash is a primary requirement for doing almost anything, including accumulating more cash. In fact the commercialism of television is a kind of guarantee of its innocence in other areas: It doesn't aim at propaganda, it doesn't define or prescribe what we should do or think. Like the rest of us, it just wants to make a living.

And indeed we know that and approve of the way it makes its living. In the main it comes free to us. Though cable and satellite put a tax on what we see, it's a small enough bite to be acceptable. We also know, of course, that though what we get through the air is free, it's not a gift. The reason we don't have to pay for the programs we watch is that the people who pay for them expect to get their money back round about as we buy the goods or services they advertise. We take this arrangement as an acceptable bargain; after all, we are going to buy *somebody's* beer and toothpaste and insurance and automobiles. In any case advertising support for the media is an old story, something else that television didn't invent.

Here in America, at any rate, the interwoven patterns of the cash nexus are a constant and central fact of life, a universal component of the world and its workings. Back BT, before television, an American president declared, "The business of America is business." The fact that television is in business, that it's the biggest medium for selling goods and services, is a reason for us to trust it. Indeed attempts to sell anything else—political ideas, social policies, or economic theories—are likely to be met with general mistrust. "Those people have something up their sleeves," we say to ourselves. But we already know what television has up its sleeve: Commercial breaks are there even if we mute them. Once the purpose of television has been defined as selling the products of its sponsors, we find it hard to believe that it can be tainted by a less forthright, more dubious motive. "Why should it be?" we ask. "What can be as important as making a living?"

All right, we can define our conscious relationship with television. TV is familiar and undemanding, distracting and companionable, it speaks of problems we know, and it does so in a generally encouraging fashion, since to refuse to treat trouble seriously does diminish it in our minds, at least for time of viewing. We don't question television's motives because we are sure we know what they are. And indeed, to continue at the level of conscious knowledge, we're right. TV programming is not dictated by a conspiracy of mad merchants intent on supporting the status quo or reversing social change, eager to turn female viewers into sex objects and males into beer-drinking, gun-toting cowboys. But the business of merchants is merchandising, and that enterprise is more easily done if roles and rules stay the same and marketers can address purchasers in a familiar, if heightened, language. Even those of us who dislike the rules and the roles relied on here or find the language ridiculous have to admit that the ads generally use the technique of persuasion to motivate us. A little shaming creeps in from time to time, but it's not irresistible.

Programs or news, what we get is a consensus view, and as long as that is persuasive and compelling, who needs a conspiracy? Merchants and programmers and ambitious advertising tycoons, producers and anchor-folk, are all at work to create a shadow world that grips the audience by reflecting human desires and responding to human wishes. Superficially the only break between that world and the one we live in is a welcome determination to play down the worries of the latter. The product, a polished if tasteless apple, needs no insinuating serpent to persuade us to accept it as a substitute for troublesome reality.

Once we do so, it's not hard for us to accept also the goods we see, shined up and magnified, that match the needs the medium tells us we feel. People in the business are good at their jobs. For them too the business of America is business; and the range of television-as-entertainment, which carries over into the commercials, is wide enough to allow inventive salesmanship to thrive. Anyway salesmanship shuns the serious, which may always turn controversial and antagonize possible buyers.

Perhaps the only things about television that should be taken seriously, then, are the consequences of creating this good-natured, affable, adaptable monster. These consequences aren't confined to the content of the programs or the style of presentation about which I spoke in the last chapter. Important as these matters are, they are not the whole story. After all, what is shown can be easily changed if, for instance, a new audience should be identified. Then new kinds of programs can be designed to reach it. The explosion of religious programming over the last decade is a case in point.

More permanent and more important because it's harder to evaluate is a built-in technological component that can't be got rid of by shifting the pictures on the screen. There sits the set, like Alice's looking glass, inviting us to go through the screen and enjoy the alternate world it displays. But in fact the screen is not just a mirror that distorts our world by eliminating the serious and shifting the significance of events and people and public matters so that, just as in Alice's dreamworld, some grow in size and some dwindle away. It is actually an impassable barrier. We can't go through the screen and talk with the people beyond it; we can only listen and look. Here is a machine for distancing agents from patients in an ultimate way. As a definer it's impenetrable to argument.

True, the separation of audience from performers is an old conventional device with which we're familiar. Not only entertainment and drama but ritual ceremonies too regularly divide participants and observers in various ways. In church the congregation responds in prescribed words at indicated times. It stands, sits, and kneels by rote. By its behavior it declares its difference from the celebrants conducting the service, its distance and its lesser status. In the theater, stage and auditorium are similarly divided from each other, like chancel and nave. At times this artistic distancing may be broken by some experimentally minded playwrights and/or directors. Characters may rush down the aisles and assault the elevated area of proper performance, others may lean out of a box in the space reserved for viewing and interrupt the dialogue. Or the audience as a whole may be invited to share in the action, to sing, move about, come up on the stage and assist the magician, and so on and so forth. But these deliberate transgressions of the audience/actor barrier in fact emphasize its existence. We understand them to be rhetorical ways of violating norms in order to create special effects. These violations don't destroy the actor/audience division; they use it to heighten the performance. It's a kind of playful improper behavior controlled by the director of the performance.

The television set hardens the space between viewers and actors into absolute separation. What looks like interaction, our response to the production we're watching, can't be heard by those who set us laughing or weeping; we're in different worlds. The people on the screen exist for us, sometimes as close and beloved companions, but the other side of the relationship has disappeared. It doesn't bother the performers. Indeed they don't seem to see the relationship in these terms. During an interview on public radio,[2] the host of a religious program, Mother Angelica, spoke with reverent delight about her closeness to the audience. They met, she said, "one on one. I can go into their living rooms and speak to them directly." The fact that they couldn't speak back (except for a few replies filtered through a telephone link controlled by the station) not only didn't disturb her; it didn't seem to enter her head.

Authority that is sure it's legitimate often thinks of interaction with its constituency in this way: "I can speak to them in person. Therefore the encounter is personal." And we should of course remember that television is not the first medium of communication to separate audience and performers completely. The movies did that first. But this older separation was mediated by taking place in a theater, and theaters imply distancing by their physical construction. Our sensitivity to the movies we see in theaters is still conditioned by the layout.

When absolute separation occurs in one's living room, the effect is different. There's an unavoidable falseness about watching an absent presence that is eerie. What kind of reality does it possess? A powerful creature, president, prophet, preacher, is speaking to us as we sit in the midst of our own surroundings—and he doesn't know he's there. What's more, he can be made to vanish in a trice, at our command. Press a button, turn a switch, the presence is gone, and it doesn't know that either. What is the relation between us made of? Does it exist in the real world? And the set is part of the real world, we find that out if it malfunctions and the hero on the screen is engulfed by fog. But what comes over the set seems more like magic, a presence that we call up ourselves as if we were invoking some ethereal or demonic spirit. At the same time, we know very well that somewhere, sometime, people really did do and say the things we're watching. They were real then—if the program is "live" they are real now—but we're not there. How then do we define the connection between us, which defies and disjoints time and space? To many of the lonely it's a very important connection. Where does it exist? Inside our heads? Certainly it's ambiguous, since it gives us an illusion of control and permits us to end the relationship by turning off the set or switching the channel; and yet this power to wipe out a performance is unfelt by the images that we have consigned to oblivion.

It seems to me that this casual, habitual action must produce some kind of interruption of our awareness of process as it exists in a world of actual people and things and events. Such a hiatus may be more truly isolating than loneliness, for it detaches us from mutual contact. We are offered a semblance of power and a degree of choice (though never the choice to invent or create what we see); we can call up a vision of actuality, we are given access to dreams that aren't our own. And all the time, in fact, we are alone. Those who speak to us so confidently and so personally, one-on-one, are speaking not only to isolated individuals, the ultimate dust of authority's capacity to divide and rule; they are speaking to the dumb. Or have they, the speakers, been rendered deaf?

The distance between viewers and performers doesn't prevent any communication at all. We can call the broadcasting station or write angry letters to the sponsor of a program we dislike. But such communication is a pale and disembodied version of actual interaction. In the past, public presentations that did not, let us say, find favor could be interrupted immediately. The timing of the protest identified the dislikable content of a play or of an actor's performance; the message was clear. An unwary dramatist, taking a bow, could be greeted with boos, as poor Henry James discovered. Cowardly gladiators, shrinking before the lions, found their fate worsened by showers of unpleasant objects. Since the audience reaction spoke directly and comprehensibly to the performance, it became participatory. If a vaudeville act didn't play in Peoria, the artiste knew it had to be remodeled, and pretty much where and why.

Today, however, no one who's bored or put off by a television program can do a thing to intervene promptly and therefore unmistakably, and since each response is individual the message is unclear, while the impact of a number of delayed protests is tiny compared to that of a large, shouting body of annoyed spectators. What was once almost a kind of conversation is now filtered through intermediaries who themselves have little to do with creating the work that has been attacked. They are interested only in the popularity of the program, of the rating it receives. The reasons for its popularity or the reverse are a matter of surmise. "They didn't like it," says the sponsor to the producer, but the central question of what "they" had to say about causes for their reaction, what triggered protest, can't be answered except by guess or by God.

What's happening? Technology, not its users, is defining the world. And yes, certainly, the medium is the message, but it is also the static and disruption of the message. It is redefining the ways that people communicate with each other and, most particularly, the relationship between speaker and listener. It is, in fact, redefining the audience. Because time and space separate us entirely from what we can look at on the tube, our capacity to participate in the nexus that once existed between actors and audience has disappeared. When we attempt to respond to what we see, we are given a new label: We are now called "critics."

That's a word disliked by all; and not only because there is still enough babbittry around for the slogan, Don't knock, boost, to be alive. More important, the label of critic implies that the commentator has had no stake in the business at hand and thus isn't entitled to complain. Critics sit on the sidelines and bad-mouth the hardworking folk who have put on this show for their benefit (or who are trying to cope with disturbances in the real world of events). Critics can be, and are, told that they have no right to speak because they have not been involved in the action that they are attacking. The label is particularly telling when it's applied to the public performance of political figures, for whom television has become so central a means of campaigning. It's easy to see here how the tag of critic diminishes the importance of any disagreement with candidates and their policies.

There's specious truth to the label, too, owing to the wall between performers and audience that is built into television. We are reduced to the role of silent observers, an audience that gazes on whatever scenario (to borrow a word favored by Nixon and company) is presented. Emotionally such distancing obscures the difference between ordinary screen divertissements and the public matters where our role is properly that of citizens, not audience. As a result we become habituated to seeing ourselves as "others," excluded from taking a hand in events that concern us. At the same time, this redefinition assists authority to see us as a mass to be acted on, a bundle of data, a collection of statistics.

How much, one wonders, has the growth of the imperial presidency in the United States over the past generation been affected by this kind of distancing between those who do and those who watch? Rulers and ruled or, to us a pleasanter phrase, authority and its citizens, are both aware that most of the public political business we see comes to us via the looking-glass barrier of the television screen. Our acceptance of the technological separation that accompanies these presentations necessarily changes the way in which each group sees the other. We the viewers, of course, don't see anything that the camera isn't focused on. As for the performers, they don't see the television audience at all. Even if some spectators are present in the flesh, they are surely outnumbered and possibly of a different political complexion than those of us watching at a distance. Overall, that is, political figures are becoming images and not flesh-and-blood presences. As the division between voters and their representatives hardens, one wonders how old ideals of democratic accountability change.

The Reagan Ascendancy has made the performance quotient of governing very clear, but performance as show (rather than performance as a means to accomplishing an end that can be a useful sort of persuasion) has played an increasingly important role in politics for some time. Eisenhower, elected to the presidency at the dawn of the television era, was the last president whose reputation was sufficient to outweigh his kindly fumbling and bumbling on the tube. In 1960, Kennedy's charismatic personality put him miles ahead of other contenders both in the primaries and in the general election for the presidency, but without the coincidence of timing that blessed him with the explosive growth of a television audience, he might have found it harder to overcome the handicap of a religion that was still felt to be "other" and his relative unfamiliarity to a nationwide audience. In the past other charismatic candidates failed to reach the White House. Bryan of the silver tongue tried three times without success. The first charismatic Roosevelt, Theodore, did not arrive at the White House on his own, but via vice-presidential service to McKinley, hardly a figure to inspire the imagination. Radio, television's precursor, certainly aided the second Roosevelt in his bid for office. But television, adding sight to sound, is enormously more potent. The actor's skills have always been important in politics, though not always commanding, even now. Richard Nixon could hardly lay claim to that advantage. But what we now see in the redefining of candidates is the increasing importance of a skilled presentation of the self. What else may this factor outweigh? Questions, I've noted, are a needed first line of defense against accepting definitions too easily. That one, raised by television, should be borne in mind.

There are many other obvious effects of the medium on politics. The expense of television advertising has helped to encourage the invention and growth of political action committees, or PACs, with their concentration on single issues. Equally candidates who command strong financial support can swamp their poorer rivals. Incumbents and challengers who have a known track record also rouse suspicions of favoritism on the part of the networks. And the vexed question of exit polling raises the issue of viewer-voter participation in another context.

This context is the decline of participation by ordinary citizens in the ongoing processes of politics, such as the active selection of candidates and open discussions of policy in old-fashioned town-meeting style, or in disputatious party gatherings. Once we the people do nothing more than say yea or nay to candidates in an election (choosing them, like TV programs, from a preselected list), the opportunity to influence affairs has already been minimized. Activism in the nomination of candidates is now largely confined to professionals or to those with a burning interest in some special issue. Even voting in primaries is sadly diminished. So the exit-poll question grows increasingly vexing. If exit polls make known to voters in the later time-zones of the West that the outcome is a foregone conclusion, the significance of their one political act disappears. Voting becomes a farce and the election itself a mere spectacle, not an event we can influence.

I don't want to suggest that this situation is beyond change. The technology of television has already loosened up some limits in its use and introduced a greater choice of programs. Cable broadcasting has not only increased the number of channels available but aimed at groups with particular interests. The introduction of videocassette recorders permits not only the taping of on-the-air programs but also the rental and purchase of cassettes in the same way that books can be bought or borrowed from libraries. Some of the figures who enter our living rooms are now there with a personal invitation from the viewer.

In a different area, interaction between producers and audiences is being demonstrated by the shop-at-home programs currently available. Goods are displayed that can be ordered directly, so that commercials and substance merge into one. One can see here the potential for audience response in a political setting. Sociologist Benjamin R. Barber has already suggested the use of television links within a locality as an extension, if not a replacement, of town meetings.[3] Some adaptation would certainly be required to adjust a system for ordering goods to one that invites discussion of policies or candidates, but when and if an experiment was made, it might very well encourage involvement in public affairs. In local settings, at any rate, issues are apt to be familiar and important in daily life. Taxes, land use, pollution, commercial development, and always questions of education policy, from textbooks through busing to the admission of pupils with AIDS to classes, have aroused heated disputes.

Valuable though such increased participation in politics would be, we still have to consider the effect of a divided and separated audience. Its members could watch proceedings and talk back to the chair or to argufiers in a central hall, but they couldn't very well talk to one another, sound one another out, and form action alliances. No contemporary Bastille is going to be stormed by observers at leisure scattered through some hundreds of living rooms. Control of the meeting would surely remain in the hands of the organization that was in charge. A certain amount of heckling is an old and important factor in political activity. But how could such improper behavior be programmed into an electronic town meeting? At what level of perceived bad manners would a heckler be cut off? If absent speakers could only be heard and not seen, would their interventions seem as significant as the contributions of the more favored folk in the hall? Would a divided audience be able to raise its own awkward questions and find friends to repeat them? Above all, how could a "sense of the meeting" grow and manifest itself if there was no meeting?

Another aspect of recent political campaigning suggests that the distance between voters and candidates, combined with the apparent familiarity we feel from their presence on the screen, is putting a premium on their turning up in the flesh. When we deplore the length of presidential campaigns today, and the narrowing of the field that their costs produce, we might also consider that the practice does bring these potential leaders into real contact with voters in many states and localities. An urge to discover what these touted figures look like up close points to some degree of revolt in the hinterlands. Iowa and New Hampshire are not great hubs of population. If early primaries and caucuses bring candidates in, the importance of these areas is of course enhanced and that's pleasant as well as profitable. But in addition the contestants become visible in human size. They have to show up and really run as part of the old, participatory political game.

True, more citizens will watch the candidates on the screen than meet them on the street, but the fact of their being there, on the street, in the same community, narrows the distances between "them" and "us." It indicates, too, that the voters are still important enough for these powerful people to seek them out and that the political relationship has not been entirely reduced to gesture and rhetoric, on the one hand, or to compliance, on the other.

But—personal appearances and unprogrammed debates are not going to offset the powerful messages delivered by careful presentation of candidates on the television screen. And the message is increasingly the person, not the agenda. Arguments and programs and campaign promises won't vanish, heaven knows, but television inevitably downplays the importance of policies in favor of the personality of the candidate. The intimacy of the medium, its transportation of all of these important people into our own living space, the illusory closeness of contact, all speak of private encounters.

We don't expect that such encounters will not be personal, will center only on public policies. Instead we stare at the person appearing before us, searching for clues to the mind, the self, the identity. Once again, it is a very old tradition that the illusion of personal interest and warmth projected by a ruler is a great part of the appeal made to the ruled. Today, when the effect is enhanced by our habit of finding companionship on the screen, the immediate figure of authority far outweighs any policies or plans. The Reagan phenomenon, of a president liked and trusted to an extraordinary degree while approval for his plans and programs runs far behind his personal popularity, is a cogent illustration of the triumph of personality over political action.

The separation of a president from the doings of his administration has happened before, but it has never been so long-lasting and so extreme as in the Reagan years. I don't think that is entirely a product of the Teflon charisma of the incumbent. Many factors feed into the effect, which is enhanced by television but hardly created by it, nor even by Reagan's expertise at playing the role of himself. The flattening of the emotional landscape, the sense of disturbing and accelerating change in the workplace and in neighborhoods, plus the lack of an overall map that would relate traditional guidelines for conduct to our current existence—all these uncertainties add to individual and social insecurity. And so we find it harder and harder to arrive at judgments about policies and programs. Large decisions of that kind ask us to think ahead, to follow a process to a likely conclusion. But how can we judge what is likely without a map we can trust? The emotional faith that we place in a person comes much more easily, and an aura of assurance goes a long way in persuading us that this confident figure knows what he or she is doing. That's a quality that Ronald Reagan has enjoyed and which his predecessor could not project. Jimmy Carter seemed to be asking for our sympathy as a representative of the common man, someone just like us. Leave out the matter of whether we in fact want to regard ourselves as common; it's certainly not what we want from a president. Franklin Roosevelt, spokesman for the common man, was never thought of as common himself.

The politics of personality are as dangerous now as they have ever been. Who do we find to lead us in times of trouble? The prime contender has been, is, and will be, the messianic emperor, hailed as inaugurator of a new age of gold; the once and future king who offers us a tapestry of dreams.

Chapter 12

TODAY'S DREAMS ARE VIOLENT.

So is reality, and each act of violence, real or imagined, feeds on the other. "Things fall apart," wrote Yeats some seventy years ago. "The center cannot hold; / Mere anarchy is loosed upon the world." Civil war at home in Ireland was duplicated and magnified by the Great War in Europe, that terminal illness of the Continent as a common civilization. Crowns and dynasties fell; national boundaries shifted and populations with them until (it must have seemed) random violence was redefining everyday life. Yeats's lines became, and have remained, a touchstone for the age of the afterquake. Prophetic and banal, they foretold and tell still a repetitious present of brutal confrontation.

Reading the poem, however, one finds that it does not speak of random violence and purposeless destruction. Instead it announces the advent of a new central power: evil, bestial, alien, but embodied nonetheless in divinity. "The Second Coming" of its title is that of a horrendous and sacred being: "A shape with lion body and the head of a man, / A gaze blank and pitiless as the sun," the "rough beast" whose hour has come round at last. It seems as if the human imagination can't tolerate a world with no center at all. Better a beast-god than nothingness. Better, one might say analogically, a black hole than meaningless galactic dust; anything but the anarchy of the poet's first vision.

It was a vision that haunted those whose world was changed by the Great War: unpredictable violence that was also a disguise for Something Else. Kafka described, in works that became another touchstone for the age, the same experience of confusion, loss, and alienation. His protagonists were caught in mysterious meanders that radiated out from another center of power. They were subject to forces derived from unknown rules. It seems as if the human need for guidelines and definitions is so great that when a familiar structure begins to disintegrate we interpret the disorder that follows less as a breakdown than as evidence of another alien authority that is projecting its own disturbing images and prescriptions into our world.

The question of power and its proper definition has been an issue of great moment since time began, both for philosophers and for practical politicians. For my purposes in this book, and in an earlier study, *Powers of the Weak,* I find it most useful to define power as a relationship between rulers and ruled and not as a quality possessed by powerful people and usable without considering reactions on the part of the ruled. Powerful people, that is, are in charge, but not automatically. They have to work at it, within the relationship that offers them the chance to direct the actions of the rest of us. They organize administrative structures, they lay out policies that they want to see implemented, and they arrange for the implementers to be monitored; but gaining their ends still calls for a process of bargaining intended to win the consent of those on the other side of the social contract. The power to define, using such instruments as persuasion and shaming, is a primary tool for enlisting the will of the governed in the service of the governors.

But as we all know, there is a third method by which authority can impose its directives, and that is *force.* In fact force as a technique of rule is so evident that it's often thought of as the only means necessary for governance. That is not the case, if only because the implementers of policy, the bureaucrats, and of force, the army and the police, can't simply be *driven* into following orders. Unless they have invested a degree of emotion in the programs of the power center they serve, they will serve it badly. Persuasion plus the possibility of shaming produces in them a personal commitment to accepted authority stronger than any degree of force could *by itself.* Nonetheless it's true to say that the right of a state to police its citizens and punish them for rule breaking is fundamental to the existence of the state; and like the Lord God, the state is jealous. It does not welcome the usurpation of its unique right to use force because that right establishes its supreme authority, though it may at times license lawbreaking, which is labeled "vigilantism." Otherwise authority regards violence that originates outside the system as directed against the system. The rest of us go along with that view. We not only agree that the state has the sole right to use force against its citizens; we hold that the use of force is a duty when "the common good" is at stake.

Let's not waste time defining "the common good" beyond saying that the name is achieved by means of persuasion and public relations exerted by whatever groups can produce the most plausible grounds for describing the ends they desire as being "good for everyone." Let us move on to explore the processes by which force operates within the power partnership.

For the powerful it has obvious attractions. Speedy obedience is one. Habituation to force minimizes any need to spell out persuasively the advantages that the governed will gain from following orders. Threats of force also cut down on the incidence of improper behavior, which can be time-consuming to deal with and may, in addition, suggest to observers that the Establishment is not in firm command. Nor does force have to be used only by official police. When stigmatization suggests its use, temporary vigilantism brings out loyal citizens ready to take hearty action against dissidents. In itself this use of force deepens the commitment of citizen to state by sanctioning what would otherwise be labeled "improper behavior," thus illustrating the power of the state.

Beating up the stigmatized, whether it's done by the

police or by enthusiastic members of the public, is a persuasive way to keep possible offenders in line. "See what can happen to you if you don't behave," says exemplary violence as it breaks shop windows, overturns cars, and burns crosses. The whole argument for the death penalty, the ultimate use of force by the civil state, hangs on the effectiveness of the example it holds up to others, since the other argument for punishment, as a means of reform, is hardly relevant when the criminal is dead.

Finally, there is of course the use of force by the state in time of war, action that is seen by authority as a duty undertaken for the common good, and which may deliver political benefits at least for a time by raising the level of patriotism and uniting the disaffected in support of authority.

Using force can also bring private rewards to those in the seats of power. They may be more dangerous than the overt justification of violence as a chosen method of rule which follows on public honors. For if the use of force awakens pleasure, it can become addictive. An obsession with using force as a political tool of course diminishes the chances that other methods to accomplish public objectives will be tried, methods that may well be more effective. Unfortunately the ability to command obedience expands the ego, and the quicker the result, the greater the high. The value that is put on immediate success today, on prompt decisions, on personal daring—all these raise the esteem in which we hold force as a tool for action. Our judgment is reinforced by the risk-taking heroes of television and the demigods of sports who assure us that "winning is the only thing." All of these responses fit into the speeded-up life that we've grown accustomed to. By the same token, the concern for quick responses dulls our interest in any consequences of our deeds that may show up farther down the road.

In spite of public benefits and private rewards for the powerful, however, the habitual use of force by authority takes a toll. It weakens the relationship between the two

TODAY'S DREAMS ARE VIOLENT

members of the power partnership because it increases the
social distance that separates them. It cuts down on the ini-
tiatIve used by those who implement decisions, a resource
that's needed badly in an unpredictable world; which means
that it's always needed. Because communications pass only
in one direction, from above down, a mass of potentially
useful information is prevented from seeping upward. Of
course a center for decision making can always gather data,
but we come back to the old question of evaluation. Who
decides what's important in the gossip and rumors and tales
of threats and subversion that come to the ears of the Establishment? Distance between rulers and ruled opens the door
to error.

Clearly the possibility of mistakes doesn't nullify the attractiveness of force in the eyes of authority. On the other
hand, if force were the only instrument needed to establish
the authority of authority, why would the powerful be wast-
ing time on persuasion and shaming? Let's look at the other
side of the power relationship: How does force work to win
consent from the governed?

At first blush the question seems ridiculous. The operation of violence by the rulers against the ruled (or indeed by
terrorist dissidents) is blindingly clear: Human beings give in
to its prescriptions because they have no alternative. "They,"
the violent, are stronger than peaceable "us." Force, enough
of it anyway, is irresistible. We take that for granted.

Ever since I started thinking about the practical workings of power, beginning with their ancient, primary form in
gender relationships, I have found that a great deal of useful
information can be gleaned by looking hard at exactly what
we take for granted. It's here that we can unearth the assumptions we accept uncritically. It's here we start to question our maps for behavior. Do the interactions they direct
as being proper and normal fit reality as it is, or have the
maps perhaps created a reality to fit themselves? And these
"normal actions": Suppose we ask not just *why* we perform

them, but *how* they operate, in the world *and* in our heads. We do indeed yield to force because we have to, but what are the processes that produce compliance? How do they work on minds as well as bodies?

In my opinion, the successful use of force involves the other instruments of definition—persuasion and shaming—and its aim is not simply to win immediate obedience. It is to posit persuasively, plausibly, the existence of a system of rule that is more powerful than the one we had accepted and internalized. Note: This system may in fact *be* the one we know, behaving in a different manner. A representative government may slide toward totalitarian dictatorship, police violence may grow more common, vigilante groups may appear: Is this the same center we once lived under, in relative tranquillity? No; but if it wears the same familiar label we may accept it. President, prime minister, chancellor, monarch—sometimes that alien other, that rough beast, appears first in this disguise. Republican Rome, welcoming a messiah as its deliverer, was not the last political system to nurture unconsciously its own betrayer.

The use of force to establish this structure is common, and in practice we the governed certainly give in. We don't want to suffer pain, imprisonment, and loss of freedom with no hope of any other end. But this loss of hope signifies the loss of a plausible alternative. We yield to force, yes, but we don't stop thinking as we do, and the familiar responses to power continue to operate. *Shame* goes with giving in. Perhaps it's the only way to survive, but it's cowardly, and we know it. So the harried mind starts looking for other reasons for compliance. *Persuasion* takes a hand. "Might," we say, "makes right."

Put that familiar tag under the light, and it illustrates exactly the vision that Yeats and Kafka, and Orwell too, perceived. Behind the violence and dread that brought us to our knees, we imagine the presence of a different structure of power, greater than what we had known before; greater because it can mishandle us. And because it is greater, doesn't it *deserve* obedience? If might makes right, we can declare that it's right, not might, that has won our allegiance. "We needs must love the highest when we see it," wrote Tennyson. I have a hunch that we often confuse "the highest" with "the most powerful." Certainly the doctrine upholding the sacredness of kings, ancient and long-lived, embodies not only the necessity of yielding to the ruler but also the virtue of doing so.

Psychologists have a term for this dependence: "identification with the aggressor." They trace its origin to the early parent-child relationship, in which our guardian giants simultaneously thwart, punish, and care for us. We love them and need them and obey them and resent the necessity of doing so. The trust we give them depends, as well, on our knowing no alternative. In time, of course, we move beyond the family system, but these first lessons stay with us and reawaken in times of trouble. They recall the attractiveness we found in the purposefulness of the powerful, those people who told us what to do when we stood abashed before the unexpected, frightened of chaos. Orders given with threats, even with blows, may seem to our adult selves ridiculous, hateful, or mad, but at the time they assure us that someone is sure of what to do. All these experiences of power, by the way, spill out familiar poetry: "Theirs not to reason why, / Theirs but to do and die." And so the Light Brigade charged to disaster in the waiting Russian lines at Balaklava. Alfred, Lord Tennyson, seems to have been fascinated by the psychology of compulsion.

Once obedience is established, the fear of shaming returns in another form: Following orders protects the order taker from responsibility. Confronting the righteous violent (and how could they be so willing to use force unless they believed in their right to do so?), we don't want to argue. Especially we don't want to argue and win, and then have to act on our own and have our mistakes shame us. The zeal of these believers is attractive. Represented on the screen, the unrepentant heroes of television and the movies awaken our envy. To the doubtful, knowing what you're doing is admirable and doing it with all your heart is even more so. Sincerity becomes a virtue in itself, a persuasive illustration of personal security.

At this point, let us return to Yeats, who saw the dangerous magnetism of certainty: "The best lack all conviction," he says sadly, "while the worst / Are full of passionate intensity." Conviction like this overrides the question of ends and means—and of results too, in a transcendent explosion of egotism that rejects the here and now. The violent are willing to die, willing to kill. The rest of us wish we could be that sure about anything.

I have to admit that violence is harder to write about than are other means of definition and prescription. In theory, civilized society disapproves of violence, and so it should by any standard of morality. Unfortunately the result is that studying violence is apt to be disapproved of too, shuffled under the rug or consigned to some special, narrow field of thought. In our culture violence occupies an ambiguous no-man's-land, rumbling ominously in the background but not addressed directly. Aristocratic systems like those that existed in feudal Europe, the Japan of the samurai, the Mexico of Aztec warriors, the Muslim world that proclaimed *jihad*, knew where they stood with violence. It was part of daily life, used, endured, taken for granted.

Comfortable bourgeois society wants to deny violence but it keeps creeping back in on the screen and on television, in thrillers, and most intimately in the nightmares we play for ourselves in our private mental projection rooms. In wartime it's exalted as heroism since the presence of a vigilant enemy raises the level of risk while emphasizing the element of altruism. In general, however, violence, at times so necessary for protection and at others the embodiment of mindless malice, defies rational evaluation. We may condemn it as the curse of an unfortunate underclass or distance it by turning it over to specialists in criminal justice or military strategy. Let these experts think about such esoteric arenas of action, we say to ourselves, much as if we were speaking of brain surgeons.

In fact we can learn a good deal about violence as a form of definition if we look at the kind of training that results in using it and enduring it as a matter of course. Coolness under attack, thinking steadily in the face of threats, is a preparation for making the decisive move at the right time in any situation. This ability is what we admire in the righteously sincere, the heroes who take up arms against injustice whom we encounter on the screen. If they are loners, with whom we who are lonely too can identify easily, our own remembered stings come to mind and we support their recklessness with envy as well as admiration. When they are shown as part of a dedicated band, we covet the loyalty that binds these daring groups together; a word that can, I guess, be defined as a nice, a proper name for "identification with the aggressor." Such loyalty merges part of the personality of the soldier/activist into the organization that controls him or her. Loyalty might also be seen as a more intense form of "consent of the governed." Possessing it, troops take pride in needing no overt persuasion to follow orders, though of course the rituals of belonging and the camaraderie of service act as forms of persuasion. Loyalty also increases the effectiveness of shame, of letting down one's comrades, and it justifies the use of force against traitors or deserters. It is the aim of all power centers.

Indeed, defining fidelity simply as a result of training for violence distorts its nature. Loyalty, risk taking, joyful participation in action, do not have to be based on the use of force. Commitment to nonviolent political action, for example, can be at least as binding and can teach courage as effectively. Gandhi and Martin Luther King grew in moral stature and in influence by their rejection of violence, in favor of another way to gain their ends. The technique that both used was *shaming*, exerted tellingly against their supposedly high-minded, Christian-indoctrinated opponents. In addition the steady resistance of their followers to violence used against them and to the temptation to indulge in it themselves proved extremely *persuasive* to many onlookers. As Gene Sharp writes in *The Politics of Nonviolent Action*,[1] resistance to force without resorting to force oneself operates as a kind of jujitsu by which violence rebounds against its users. It acts out a drama in which the attackers are shamed before the eyes of a broad citizen-audience and the courage, sincerity, and sureness of the resisters invites public admiration. The ability to act the part, however, requires not only commitment and courage but a deep habituation to endurance and a great deal of political sophistication, among followers as well as leaders.

Most of us don't have such resources. Looking at violence, we think of ourselves as lone victims, and as lone victims we see no alternative to obeying orders. We lack the vision of a variant power center to which we can adhere, in which we can find strength. Not force itself, but force as credible evidence of another way of defining the world and acting on the prescriptions that follow, swings us toward accepting a new, or ratifying a familiar but altered, structure of power.

Putting the use of force into this context should help us evaluate the spreading violence of our time. It suggests that terror is never as strong an instrument of the state as it claims to be, and that terrorism is not a random and mindless phenomenon. State terror presents the regime it serves as being unchallengeable; no behavior is permitted here but proper behavior. But, as I've been saying, improper behavior is seldom the product of plan. It happens because old rules for propriety are breaking down. They are violated unintentionally, out of a need for survival or simply for efficiency.

What happens then? Does terror engulf the naïve, if errant citizens? Does the state tighten its rules and hold to its old prescriptions? Well, if they were breaking down in the first place, enforcing them more stringently won't make them any more useful. This state is losing, not gaining, control over reality and its shifting demands. Sooner or later some better-organized and more pragmatic structure of power is going to appear from within or without. Other things being equal, a flexible and inventive political center is going to beat a rigid structure dominated by the past.

As for the frightening randomness of terrorism with its propensity for hitting out at innocent bystanders—this randomness is purposive. Terrorism wants to discredit the ability of the regime it's attacking to maintain order. So it creates disorder. Responding to it with violence produces more disorder. "Fine," says terrorism, "you're playing our game." Which side has more to lose, after all? The terrorists, or the state that is charged with preserving tranquillity?

These two sorts of political violence, that used by the state and that which attacks it, occupy the extremes. It's not surprising that what they share, a commitment to force as the ultimate persuader, produces mutual understanding. At times it becomes collusion, as political police infiltrate revolutionary cells and revolutionaries penetrate and seduce the Establishment. A century or so ago this kind of interactive betrayal was at least as common as thriller writers make it seem today. The best-known episode involves the head of the tsarist secret police who not only funded the writings of the Social Revolutionaries who advocated "direct action," that is, violence, but managed to arrange for them to assassinate a cousin of the tsar, the grand duke Sergei, and the minister of the interior, to whom the police reported. These deaths certainly made the political police seem vitally important, and emphasized the need to fund them well! Provocation of this kind is familiar and tempting; FBI scams have caught greedy millionaires and ambitious politicians. When it's joined to a willingness to use violence, its dangers became more apparent: The means distort the end, the instrument assumes more importance than its purpose and inevitably faith in the cause weakens in the minds of the manipulators. True, the private soldiers of terrorist organizations remain more devout, willing to kill, willing to die, loyal—but expendable. For the manipulators their martyrdom has great value. Like the death penalty, it's exemplary: This cause must be powerful and its promises satisfying if its followers are ready to face death.

A third sort of political violence, vigilantism, is more instructive because it's less extreme and closer to commonplace experience. It grows out of muddled situations where power centers and value systems contend but where lines between the state and the dissident activists aren't clearly drawn. In their book, *Vigilante Politics,* H. Jon Rosenbaum and Peter C. Sederberg speak of it as a kind of "boundary maintenance" used by one social group against challengers when firm control by a central power structure is lacking.[2]

This nongovernmental use of violence that is still licensed by authority has been a frequent response to—and example of—improper behavior in America. In one of the essays included in *Vigilante Politics,* historian Richard Maxwell Brown has identified "at least 326 vigilante movements or episodes" in the period 1767 to 1910.[3] The count since then is not given, but the Ku Klux Klan, for example, has been born, and reborn, and born again. In 1986 *The New York Times* reported that soldiers and marines stationed in North Carolina had been attending meetings of a white supremacist organization known till recently as the Carolina Knights of the Ku Klux Klan.[4] In June of the same year, National Public Radio noted a rumor that a cell of the Klan, connected to the Baltimore "Klavern," was operating at CIA headquarters.[5] Now, the Army and the Marine Corps were not about to use force to maintain the boundaries of white supremacy in 1986; and the motives of the CIA are too cloudy for the civilian mind to penetrate; but the survival, and the continuing outreach, of this instrument of definition-by-force were demonstrated by the rock-throwing response of white supremacists in Forsyth County, Georgia, on the birthday of Martin Luther King in January 1987.

If vigilantism is often defined as "establishment violence," it also occurs in situations where its actions question the legitimacy of a government. The Nazi violence in the streets that preceded Hitler's takeover can be labeled "vigilantism," though Hitler was attacking the existing democratic German government. His support came from elements of both the Right and the Left, not only those who wanted to keep what they had but those who wanted more. As his influence grew, his Brown Shirts found official allies until, with his assumption of the post of chancellor, this violence was fully licensed by the state. At that point it merged into state terror.

In fact none of these labels for political violence—terrorism, state terror or vigilantism—is ever exact or permanent. The confused social conditions in which vigilantism takes root are especially subject to change. So is the nature of this amorphous hostility, which can vanish if authority takes over with a firm hand, and can arise anywhere, anytime, authority fails to exert control. Speaking sociologese, Rosenbaum and Sederberg label this condition "regime ineffectiveness." We can find historical analogies in the birth of feudalism, as powerful local barons took over the prerogatives of rule from a weak monarchy, and in the periods when Chinese emperors gave way to warlords. Force is what we see first, but what's in dispute is exactly the power to define. What the barons gained in the early Middle Ages was the right to tax, to hold their own courts and inflict punishment by their own rules, to control property and its inheritance, and to raise armed men. Here are all the instruments of definition bound up together, from labeling to prescriptions enforced by violence. They are the heart of the matter.

If we look back at Klan vigilantism in our own history, we don't find a weak central government as a precipitating cause, but rather a muddled one. Once defeated, the Confederate South was never going to rise again in arms. Overt, sanctioned slavery was dead, but the definition of the proper status of black people, of their rights and entitlements, was far from settled. The southern vision was hardening, as we've seen: "darkies" into "niggers" as the labels reflected the shift from a definition that emphasized childishness to one that put alien otherness first. In the victorious North, a moral commitment to equality had produced the post–Civil War constitutional amendments, which freed black slaves, gave them the right to vote, and announced "equality." But ten years of occupation under Reconstruction had been expensive, in money and in general turmoil. Ruling the states of the old Confederacy ceased to be a matter of principle and became a practical problem in politics. The North cut a deal. The troops withdrew, the amendments stayed on the books, and the Klan, born in the first years of turmoil, revived.

Here were the heirs of the old southern power structure, frustrated, ambitious and violent, ready to exert their right to define the status of black people by any means available. The whole exercise is a case study in definition into prescriptions and enforcement. Direct violence increased, but indirect violence by means of definition supplemented it: Discrimination was legalized by passage of the Jim Crow laws, which declared that offenses against white supremacy were illegal. A legal system that turned a blind eye to lynching and arson now gave the white courts power to label blacks criminals if they infringed on the color line.

Shaming and propaganda played their part too. "Nigger lovers"—they might be whites who disapproved of lynching—were subject to shaming. The vision of pure white womanhood was exploited to persuade the tolerant of the danger of rape. And behind it all lingered the myth of a tranquil golden age of racial peace and courtesy, existing in the old times, before the war.

Repression in the South had a long life in contrast to the vigilantism on the frontier. There roving bands of adventurers menaced property and life in territory where ownership of land and resources had not been settled or political control established. "Frontiersmen," writes Richard Maxwell Brown, "ordinarily desire new opportunities but not social innovation." When "lower people and outlaws wished to burst their lower-level and fringe boundaries," and thus upset the social structure, they ran into the determination of "men of upper-level background or aspirations . . . to reestablish the community structure in which they were ascendant." A contemporary observer describes the process: "The honest people [were] trying to expel the others by the terrors of the law, and when that mode failed, forming *regulating* (vigilante) companies and driving them out by force."[6]

There are many ways of describing this phenomenon: as popular justice determined to establish law and order; as a natural response to a political vacuum where even "decent men" could oppose each other over land use; and as "socially constructive" community organization, though Brown points out that "even the best vigilante movements usually attracted a fringe of sadists and naturally violent types, [while] sadistic punishment and torture, arbitrary . . . killings and mob tyranny marked vigilante movements that had gone truly bad."[7] In the absence of a political structure that can moderate passionate intensity and broker the requirements and desires of different groups, ad-lib popular justice takes over. What brought an end to frontier vigilantism by 1900 was the steady western drive of ordinary government and regular legal proceedings. They provided no utopia but they were reasonably efficient and at least minimally open to "lower people." The established system outdid and outbid the ramshackle alternative that vigilantism had created.

In the South, however, Jim Crow and Klan violence

hung on for something like a century. The corpse of the old white supremacy lay across a land of poverty and dreams, and the defeat of the Confederacy was not ratified in daily existence by actual social changes. The beginning of the end—the end has not yet been reached—came as part of a slow, deep, apparently unrelated revolution that changed the conditions of life. After World War II, and spurred by the economic development in new areas that the war precipitated, commercial and industrial investment moved south. The old, mythic structure began to break down, and modified arrangements for living between classes and races became imaginable. Black people took advantage of these opportunities, as they had in Reconstruction days, and the civil rights movement invoked the law and order that the federal government had not tried to enforce since 1876. As black people firmly redefined themselves and their public status, vigilantism declined. Once more, no utopia, but a potential divergence from entrenched injustice resulted.

All sorts of violence confront Western civilization if, indeed, one can still give it this label. Angry groups based on class or race or religion or a combination of causes have begun to define "us," rather than the other way around. To our surprise they label us as undesirable aliens. Our culture is losing the persuasive allure we had assumed it would always exert. We saw ourselves as offering a progressive democratic alternative to ancient bloody tyranny and all at once the latter choice is attracting adherents. The machinery and the material goods that we had so heartily defined as providing solid grounds for "the good life" are still desired by many, but the desire itself has overturned social structures in other parts of the globe, bringing famine to the countryside and desperate poverty to the expanding cities. And we don't know what to do about it any more than we do about the manmade apocalypse that we have contrived to invent as a possible final solution for all our arguments and opportunities and visions.

These remarks seem very distant, I'm sure, from the troubled patient in the first chapter, asking the doctor to name and prescribe for his ailments. But when we are talking about power and its uses and its unexpected consequences, its failures and its more dangerous triumphs, we are talking about a process that runs the gamut from private life into the political sphere. A troubled individual and a troubled society ask the same kind of questions, hoping for directions that will ease our anxieties and maybe, just maybe, show us a road to health.

In these hopeful moods we dare to look for ways to improve the workings of the power relationship, and indeed the adventures in change that Western civilization has undertaken and survived provide examples. The category of those citizens who can be defined as important enough to be listened to on matters of culture and politics and public affairs has grown substantially. In America the last couple of generations have seen an increasing recognition of the values that a century and a half of immigration have imported. Writing, music, and art from many backgrounds have poured into our traditional WASP culture, enriched it, and made familiar the bearers of these new ways of seeing and doing. This kind of establishment of a group's presence also increases its participation on the scene of political power. Newcomers cease to be alien, and social distances narrow.

This experience differs from the smug nineteenth-century ideal of a melting pot, which assumed that all changes would be made by the new arrivals. Early on, capable and ambitious newcomers do often find themselves forced into the role of "tokens." They have to abandon their backgrounds or occasionally act out some salient feature of customary behavior, the sort that's known to the Establishment and will identify these incomers *as* incomers. Individual access to a place on the hierarchical ladder doesn't raise the status of a token and his/her people; instead it confirms them as outsiders because tokens have to leave their origins behind. Only when a group is revalued does the cultural background of its members become part of the accepted store of wisdom that a society calls on for directives to proper action. The United States has watched with a mixture of astonishment, resentment, and pride the entrance of Irish and Jews, Italians and eastern Europeans, Hispanics and Asians, into full citizenship in a nation that once assumed that white Anglo-Saxondom was the fount of all wisdom.

A couple of other groups have had harder going: blacks and Native Americans. In part the perception of body differences sets up roadblocks, but I think there is another, more profound case for the difficulty that authority still feels in accepting these people as "normal." Ancient guilt is part of it; white authority either stole the land from the ancestors of these people, or else it stole the ancestors themselves, who "immigrated" as slaves. I suspect that another factor is present too, one that also plays a part in the situation of women, those unexpected claimants to a piece of the pie of power. There are similarities in the way that these particular groups are seen by the white male power structure that make them less easy to assimilate, because none of us are incomers.

The universal presence of gender roles, for example, doesn't exclude women from membership in a society, but simply from areas within it. Where immigrants to a new land bring experience from outside, women don't. We've been living "right here," wherever "here" may be, and though we are generally assigned a place within our community and are understood to perform special tasks, it's assumed that the body of custom and the premises underlying morals and manners are held in common with our fathers and brothers and husbands and lovers, and now with our employers and colleagues. We're expected to behave differently but nevertheless to have assimilated the ethics and values of our native place well enough to pass them on to our sons as well as to our daughters.

Once authority has begun to entertain the possibility that immigrants from other societies can provide suggestions for dealing with reality out of their different experience, these newcomers are on their way to joining, and to altering, the mainstream political and economic structure. But what can women have to offer that is new? The Establishment isn't much interested in information from our part of the woods. Either it's old stuff or it's good only for females, whose natures are different and status inferior. Blacks and Native Americans share this situation to a considerable degree: They are conquered peoples whose cultural differences are felt to offer little that's relevant to contemporary life. What was learned in the nursery or the black ghetto or on distant reservations doesn't present itself to authority as helpful in the mainstream world.

Instead we've been invited to stay within our own cultural bounds, which means identifying ourselves as strangers. This directive is weakening, but women are still assured that they are most welcome when they indicate that they have not abandoned all the traditional role behavior that marks us as feminine. Women in the workplace know very well that there are contradictory expectations held by those they work with. Sometimes they must behave like men, sometimes like women. Ceremonial gestures to the old status relationship have to be made at the proper time and knowing the proper time is up to the woman. Black men don't face the same requirement to recall past inferiority, but the part of their lived experience that isn't familiar to whites is best suppressed. Where women can suggest that the traditional male/female relationship was and is pleasant, any reference by black people to the old white supremacy is highly embarrassing. Fortunately white and black men have the great subject of sports to bring them together without raising dubious questions of superiority. Black women may well have most freedom in contacts with white men because old types of relationship (nurse, servant, or sexual partner) are understood to be out-of-bounds in a business setting. New circumstances call for new attitudes. Native Americans profit from the same kind of existing difference; old relationships weren't close and have left few recognizable traces. Like black men, however, native Americans can seldom make easy reference to any experience that is specifically alien to white norms. That leaves a lot of early roots and character-shaping to silence; just as women's early training in female behavior—in the need to please, in charming femininity, and so on—doesn't get into conversation much.

And yet all of us who come from different backgrounds within the same society have a lot of information to pass on. But such knowledge is not, like the tips on variant ways of doing things that immigrants bring, simply addenda. It is not emotionally neutral. The lessons it provides ask for unlearning "normal" procedures and deconstructing maps. The behavior men expect from women, and often get, follows a causality that doesn't match that of men. Many women want to get away from this causality too; we don't want to get our rational points across by "feminine wiles" or win promotion by pleasing flattery. But that's what our grandmothers and mothers (and some of us, too) learned to do. It would be nice if men and women could unlearn these things together, but it often seems to men that such a prescription involves revaluing important cornerstones of comfortable society. Their own traditional learning, after all, has included the vision of two sorts of women, attractive and not. If you take that division below the surface, it is apt to strengthen and project a picture of "real women," who like men and enjoy being with them, and an opposite group of manhaters, feminist lesbian harpies who would like to do away with men entirely. It's not easy to contradict this version of the castration complex either, since it's hardly a subject for congenial conversation, and the image has long existed in popular culture.

In short, women moving away from traditional roles still present a challenge to men in spite of all the changes that have occurred in the last twenty years. There had been plenty of change before that too, but it had not been articulated. The challenge isn't confined to men either, for most women have changed the work they do and the way they live and the norms they take for granted without very much conscious evaluation. Most of us whose lives have taken unexpected directions as female participation in the paid labor force has grown, to the point where it is now taken for granted, haven't the faintest intention of attacking the overall social, cultural, and economic structure. The forces operating in this interlocking system that made it necessary or advisable for women to move into the cash economy instead of working only in family settings did not present themselves as sweeping social demands but as individual, personal needs or ambitions. Like Charlie Chaplin in *Modern Times* we've found ourselves part of a totally unexpected parade that swept around the corner and gathered us up. Trying to understand what has been happening and to figure out what to do about the consequences have been literally a matter of on-the-job learning. We've acted in response to circumstances and not because of an ideology or philosophy. We have behaved improperly simply because the definitions of propriety were becoming irrelevant to the demands of everyday life.

One of the theses of this book, please recall one last time, is that individual behavior will adapt itself to changed circumstances long before the maps we use to explain the world will adjust themselves and even longer before the web of concepts that these maps reflect is rejected as being out-of-date. This period of transition is wearing. Definitions are losing a portion of their unquestionable authority and the loss invites arguments and mistrust between the argufiers. Such disputes are bad enough when they deal only with abstract ideas, but disagreement about relations between the sexes is a very slippery subject. Try as we may to discuss objectively the way that power operates within gender roles, we keep running into the fact that in real life "gender" isn't a topic for objective study. Relations between men and women are personal and if they're intimate, they're highly emotional. Public words don't fit private feelings. Speaking in the abstract, one can say quite truthfully that women's experience of power has been learned largely from male dominance; where else could it have been learned? Whatever class and race divergences exist, top cats are tom cats. If female members of the elite get a taste for practicing dominance, the opportunity is theirs because they are adjuncts of powerful males.

But just because this gender dominance operates both publicly and privately, its questioning by women is felt, on the masculine side, not as a political difference of opinion, but much more acutely, as a private betrayal of intimacy. Sex and gender, private and public involvements, love and resentment and the kinds of manipulation of position and feelings learned from different experiences of life, all confuse possible discussion: "I'm not talking about *you*," says a woman with desperate sincerity, "I'm talking about *patriarchy*."

"What the devil do I have to do with patriarchy?" the male discussant is likely to ask himself, a personal response to a statement that aimed at labeling the exchange as objective.

What does the female say if, not improbably, he says it out loud? Does she set about explaining the ramifications of the word "patriarchy"? Or does she answer, "Nothing, I hope," and thus retreat from abstract arguments into the private world that is hers by tradition?

In that case, thinks he, why are we talking about it? In the other case, how long, one wonders, is an objective exposition of the meaning of "patriarchy" going to continue? The male is going to say, pretty quickly, "But I don't feel that way about you. I don't act that way. Why are you blaming me?" Some kind of unexpected and uncalled-for judgment on the workings of the world in general, no doubt sincere but wildly out of place in any intimate connection, is showering him with undeserved shame.

That question goes to the heart of the problem. It's rooted in the perplexing confrontation with external, social change that is forced on individuals when proper behavior, defined by customary rules, loses its relevance and its effectiveness. Difficult as the situation is for ordinary people, the challenge to those in authority is greater. The right to define implies a duty to define. But if the Establishment is satisfied with things as they are, redefinition is not easy. To authority, any demand to redraw social maps originates elsewhere. It comes from the rest of humanity, not out of the experience of authority's own top people. Top people are for once being asked to think their way into the minds of those who have been defined as children, or as "others." Improper behavior has to be examined as if it were serious! "We" have to explore the not very coherent requirements of "them."

In our time, demands for new status have cropped up all over. A startled Establishment finds itself blamed for following rules that are now redefined by others as a product of racism or sexism. What seemed at the time perfectly proper behavior has suddenly been redefined as wrongful conduct whose wrongs must be redressed by action, "affirmative action." Like the male disputant cited above, reluctant managements and local institutions expostulate, "But I didn't start this. It's not my fault. Why should people pay now for what happened back then? We aren't responsible for the past. It's not fair." Public and private, political and personal events are all being scrambled together as proper behavior is relabeled.

It wouldn't be fair, that's right, if we were starting from scratch. Neither was oppression fair, whenever it might have started. Change has to start somewhere, though, if it's needed, and it starts in the present because that's the place we live in. On the other hand, if we don't look beyond the present we lose touch with the process that shaped the relationship that needs changing. We lose the past, and we lose the future too. The present isn't static; it's a moving stage full of interacting, desirous, angry human beings. The ones who like it here want things to stay the way they are, but change is happening anyway. It will override definitions and confound prescriptions whether we like it or not. The present is where we start, not where we can hope to end.

Pleas for fairness are heard around the world, made most loudly by violent activists, confronting each other with accusations of blame and all denying any part in creating disorder: Christians, Muslims, and Druse in Lebanon, Arabs and Jews in Israel, Catholics and Protestants in Ulster, and so many other people in other places, all furiously hoping and striving for what they deem to be "fair" and justifying the grisly means they use to pursue this goal by the label they give it. Where persuasion failed so long ago that it's not just forgotten, it's discredited; where shaming has no force because these enemies are so distant that they care not at all for the opinions of their opponents; then violence takes over as a means of establishing peace and proper behavior. Logically, objectively, one wants to ask, "What can violence have to do with propriety, with minding one's own business in an atmosphere of mutual respect? Why must we kill each other in order that life may be lived quietly? How strange, how confusing, that ends and means have to contradict each other!"

A woman, a feminist at any rate, would say that this terrible confusion may well be the inevitable, sad result of patriarchy, the oldest way of all to create order in the world—by splitting humanity into "us" and "them." On this primal division by gender complex hierarchical structures may rise that assure their denizens a place in the social structure but also reserve power to the powerful. Behind the vertical map of rank and status, the polarization of power is always present. . . . No, let me say it differently. The polarization of power *has always been* present. Let us not assume that such an "always" must continue forever. For polarization and its system of placement by higher and lower levels, with all the lower, of course, occupied by "them," could quite conceivably be replaced one day by a level map where difference and equality could co-exist. It's not logic but the habit of ranking that misleads us to think that such an alternative is impossible.

For now, however, we stand in a different and divided place. Because humanity makes its primary and most intense division by gender, with the public world and its management assigned to men, it is men on whom devolves the right and the duty to define the world's composition as a first step toward action, and then to persuade and stigmatize and use violence in order to accomplish whatever action is needed. In theory, forceful action is needed—and justified—in order to protect the community from attack, the women from rape, the children from abuse or kidnapping, the general populace from starvation, enslavement or murder—but what happens if a sullen people doesn't agree with orders from authority as to proper conduct? How does the Establishment make its decisions stick? When push comes to shove, we all know that we're in for a shoving. The police use force, the national guard turns out to break any strike that threatens the National Interest, civil rights are suspended and concerned citizens take up arms to defend themselves, their families, and the water supply.

What do you have then? Vigilantism? Civil war? Whatever it's called, you have violence that is not directed against external enemies. The obligation to use force in the face of danger extends to its use against a population that doesn't obey orders. Dividing the world in two and granting power in public affairs to only one segment invites—demands—oppression. How can responsible authority let the judgment of the irresponsible influence its activity?

For women, even for those who have thought hard about gender roles and the demands they make, it's damned hard to see the duty to rule, by force if necessary, as a *duty*. It looks to us more like a privilege, like a free gift of free choice and a chance to try out ideas in action on the basis of one's own decisions. We have heard quite a bit, after all, about the obligations that men take on for the benefit of those dependent on them, and a pool of black humor exists for defining such benevolence in distinctly different terms. Tell us that a good spanking hurts the spanker more than the spanked and we beg leave to doubt it.

But in fact all roles are limiting. That of ruler/decision maker is hard to evade because of the privileges it grants, but also because of the demands it makes. Men who reject power and the advantages that go with it must explain themselves: Aren't they turning it down because they're afraid of "acting like a man"? Why else would they refuse? In a polarized world one doesn't let the chance to be hailed as a hero go by without incurring the reputation of being a coward. If you won't act like a man you'll be accused of acting like a woman. When Edward VIII abdicated his throne for the woman he loved, he did not merely cease to be king. His whole image changed. He was no longer a serious, responsible, properly masculine figure but a pathetic little creature directed by the whims of his duchess.

So the choices open to men, seen through the lens of tradition, are narrow: either respected adult or frivolous dropout. The role is harshly defined. Its adherents must mediate public dangers and accept risk as part of the day's work, including the risk of making the wrong decisions, for which they alone will bear the brunt of shame. Pride and honor depend on accepting the onerous job of ruling and ordering, defining and prescribing activities that are always visible. In private, since the family takes its social position from its male head, or always has until these uncertain times, failure of the father figure extends to those he's charged with protecting.

Look at it this way and the masculine role becomes a terrible burden while shirking the job is a deplorable lapse from duty. Any privileges that go with the obligation hardly make up for its difficulties, while dissent and disobedience easily come to appear like the "ingratitude" of the freed slaves who forgot the "lenity" of their masters.

But in our time dissent and disobedience have become rife. When women began to label the care and safekeeping they had enjoyed with the name "oppression," many good men were truly shocked. Over the last twenty years the shock has hardened into resentment, which then justifies itself by declaring that women's redefinition is evidence per se of their foolishness and need for care. They condemn themselves of incompetence out of their own mouths. If they want to get on by themselves, then (says the Male Establishment, though certainly not all men) let them try it. Let them take on responsibility for managing their lives in the public world and see how they like it.

Who could deny that demands for equality carry with them responsibility for action, action that cannot be only selfish? Yet that noble gesture is not always accepted eagerly by women. Well, there are good reasons as well as bad for this reluctance. Let's put aside the two familiar restraints: the habituation to *not* being active and responsible in the public world, and the demands that the traditional female role still lays on women. The latter provides true emotional rewards; the former makes hesitation realistic. Instead let's consider the essential meaning of responsibility when it's handed to immigrants into new conditions of life, and, too, the behavior that redefining "responsibility" prescribes.

The old definition works out as authority's way of managing the world. Patriarchal society, including many women, is dubious about women as managers of society since, in this view, we would be operating by methods designed to fit the male role. We can be persuasive, that's true. We can certainly stigmatize those who fall away from proper behavior; like all those who don't hold power we often do so in order to please our masters. But can we act when hard choices must be made? That is not so certain. We've been praised for expertise in the female role of mother and nurturer and assured that we're fitted for it by our genetic heritage. And we've heard a lot about the problems of "acting like a man."

Listening to definitions, in fact, is discouraging. Our first support for action comes from behavior, past and present. Women have made hard choices and survived over the centuries, and today the mythic image of woman-as-dependent is fading through the example of those who have taken on responsibility for managing affairs and are doing it well. The last twenty years have seen drastic changes in public estimates of women's natural abilities. Such altered definitions did not take place because of argument; they were demonstrated by deeds too clearly for mistakes to be possible. Women have not been reluctant to act individually and professionally in public settings, nor have we hesitated to set up agendas for programs to aid women in general, economically, politically, or in matters of education. What we have not undertaken, however, is the construction of a system designed to deal with overall human problems. We haven't mounted a political party with goals that go beyond the social changes that would bring equality closer. Some of us have certainly imagined a society altered by revolution but the desired ends have always been the main concern, not the means of achieving them. Here the impact of women's old position has invited us to accept simplistically the inevitability of a polarized world. There is nothing wrong with the aims that feminists have enunciated, either ultimate or immediate, except that we have tended to think forward almost exclusively with women only in mind.

That's modest of us and practical too, but after twenty years of progress we might try a bit of purposive dreaming that goes beyond denying traditional definitions of women's place. It may be time to start redefining the management of public affairs in man's world in ways that don't take polarization for granted. We have been proving in practice that the premises for gender separation are often faulty. How might all this that we've learned apply to a society that is not split in two?

We'd have to expect a barrage of angry propaganda. Some of it would grow out of the split itself. We'd be told that we still don't know enough about the great public sphere to run it or repair it, that it's impossible for us not to put female interests first now that as feminists we've learned to be selfish. Chiefly we'd be told that it's impossible for other methods of management to be effective. They never have been, have they?

The serious answer to that question is simple. Never before has there been a chance to build a world that isn't split by gender. But today we have seen that jobs formerly performed only by men can be done by women. We know that mechanical tools have nullified the premiums on muscular strength that used to exist; we know that women's lives have been altered profoundly by medical science, the ability to control and limit family size, and the extension of the lifespan. Bearing children is our job and our joy, but pregnancy seldom has to be a serious interruption in a busy life and since children no longer die early from epidemic or endemic disease, fewer births are needed to maintain a population, or a family. We are still caught in the role conflict between duties in the domestic sphere and responsibilities in public matters, but the very attention that these conflicts receive is a sign of progress toward solutions. Work outside the home versus work inside it has never before commanded the public concern it raises today.

Another kind of deterrent to women-thinking-for-humanity would certainly label such efforts as hopelessly utopian and idealistic, just the kind of silly ideas that protected women are subject to. "We can't waste time on pipe dreams of universal peace and community," says the Establishment. "You really ought to know better if you want us to see you as capable colleagues in coping with world problems, in dealing with the communist enemy and terrorism and trade deficits and budget shortfalls and labor disputes." And it's certainly true that although utopian yearnings have sprung up in the hearts of men as well as women, they have seldom worked for any length of time, and even then only in closed communities. Authority recognizes their allure but has contained it through the familiar device of distancing: Utopia is an enticing aim for the distant future. Or it is moved to another world entirely. Read about it in Dante's *Paradiso* or in the more optimistic works of science fiction. Here, in our rough time, a sense of wholeness, of shared community, comes to us only in brief snatches, created by ceremonies or, mockingly, · by drug-induced euphoria. What's different today?

One thing that's different is exactly the growing diversity of cultures and of experience that is feeding into the world. Behavior once not just improper but unthinkable has already bent some standard rules for managing public affairs. When the American auto industry, brainchild of a proud tradition of homegrown mechanical skills, starts trying out methods that reflect Japanese styles of management, it appears that fear of diversity is diminishing. Not just the work force but the workplace itself is becoming heterogeneous in concepts as well as practice.

The value in such a melding of cultures is the way that pluralism works to decrease polarization and to contradict in everyday fashion the binary division of "us" and "them" with its implicit directives for confrontation. There is nothing utopian about such experiments. On the contrary they begin with pragmatics, not with the conceptual constructs that have shaped past efforts at establishing new communities. When rules for creating an ideal and perfect state are laid down in advance no room is left for alterations. Demands for adjustments are labeled dissent or even heresy. The special communities that have survived from past times have either found a way to compromise with the larger society that surrounds them, as the Mormons have successfully done, or, like the Catholic orders, they have made for themselves a valued and recognized place within this society. Even so, interaction between any set-apart group and the rest of the world is limited.

The women's movement or question or problem, and the critical intellectual elements within it, have grown out of pragmatic, behavioral change in the processes and structure of daily life. Therein lies feminism's greatest strength. Of course these shifts affect humanity, not just women. We are, however, the largest group of humans touched by change, much of our experience is common to all women, and we are making the longest journey, from ancient traditional dependence to participation in mainstream existence. It seems to me both inevitable and proper that our knowledge of the "place" we come from, and of living through the tough demands that social and cultural revolution makes on us, gives us an ability to think about alternative ways of dealing with the world that have never before been taken seriously as realistic—and yet have been the basis of the private world. We have indeed been nurturers.

The word is more than a label to us; it is an experience. We know the how and the why of it. We have been charged with monitoring and maintaining the emotional balance of a family and a household and can see how such maintenance binds different sorts and conditions of people together. We've had to figure out how to get along without simply giving orders that will be obeyed. All of this useful information can be learned, and all of it prescribes ways to manage a group that do not distance people from one another; nor does it insist on there being just one right way to behave and one proper status for each of us.

The first impulsive wave of revived feminism, starting in the 1960s and rising in visibility and acceptance through the seventies, accomplished a fair amount of adjustment in perceived gender roles. It ran into opposition as it began to challenge the underlying premises of polarization between the sexes and was countered intellectually by arguments that accused feminism itself of polarization. Feminists are supposed to be interested only in what's good for women, and particularly in what's good for women in terms of male values: success, making it, beating the boys at their own game, and as a corollary neglecting the interests of women who don't want to move out of women's traditional place. Such labeling is a useful ploy for the power to define, a version of blaming the victim. In this case, the people blamed are the women who responded to change by shifting their behavior, by going to work outside the home when work at home became less necessary and more isolating, when money demands grew heavier with changes in the economic infrastructure. What today's situation asks of feminists are critical counterarguments that are not based only on women's experiences, but on contemporary shifts in society as a whole. It's time to take a long look at the improper behavior we've been demonstrating and to read the messages that it conveys.

Improper behavior isn't right in itself any more than it's necessarily wrong. But if it persists and increases, it's *significant*. It represents today's reactions to yesterday's rules. Come back to the doctor's office where this book began. In order to treat the patient, the physician must consider the symptoms that the patient displays, the improper behavior of the body. In order to deal with social problems, we have to look at the likely causes, the friction between traditional prescriptions for living comfortably and the current demands of reality. Our diagnosis must include the rules as well as the behavior. But in fact the behavior may well be more important.

In the first place, it is responsive to change, which means that it both indicates that changes are taking place and also records human reactions to them. Those reactions can be instructive. They may point to possible solutions. At any rate they show where strain is most disruptive. Beyond the information that a power structure can gain from looking at challenges to rules, however, is the intuitive information that the rest of us acquire by living out our reactions. Minority peoples know a lot more about their needs and certainly about the contributions they can make to society in the large than does the Establishment. Since half of all minorities are female, the things that these groups have learned filter into the experience of women who are closer to what authority thinks of as "normal": in this society as white and middle-class. If women can see ourselves as a group large enough to contain and profit from the lives of all women, we become a storehouse of information about pluralistic responses to change. Pluralism is and should be a characteristic of feminism. Not only does it oppose polarization, but in a curious way it is a binding force. People who can accept diversity as a resource lose the fear of strangers that prevents our seeing common interests.

Thinking into the future today, in a time of change as substantial as our own, is terribly difficult. We are patients as well as doctors, patients with heightened emotions and rather confused minds and doctors with a profound sense of ignorance. Conditioned by roles and rules, we're not sure what's worth saving and what's harmful, yet we know that treatment for the world's problems has to start right now. How do we begin?

It seems to me that our best hope is to look at the range of improper behavior that plagues our society and try to evaluate these symptoms. They are here and present and pressing but they represent processes that have their roots in the past, so we do indeed need to think back in time and ask what's different now from the world in which these ways of managing worked. I think we must also question the great superstructure of mythic concepts that we have inherited from the past, in order to remake it. Asking those questions can be distressing because that past has provided the premises for our own actions. And yet, here we are, acting improperly. Something must have come adrift. I think, in short, that we have to interpret what we do in order to know what we ought to think and plan; which is, I guess, a standard female response to a troubling situation and one that is condemned out of hand by male philosophers. To me, and I think to many women, it means looking at the evidence before you jump to conclusions.

Evidence based on behavior is both humanistic and pluralistic. Where proper conduct reproduces known approaches to encounters and relations, unexpected activity can bring to our attention shifts in the normal course of affairs. Such unwelcome heralds of a nascent world are likely to disturb us by the bad manners, questionable morals, and unorthodox theories that they produce, but we dismiss them at our peril. In the rough passage that we're making from past to future, understanding novelty is vital even if in the end we dismiss much of it. This disorder is a form of communication from the Goddess of the Reality Principle to humanity.

When good Dr. Freud undertook his self-analysis ninety-odd years ago, it was an act of great bravery. We may well differ from his interpretation of what he discovered. After all, the cultural maps he used differ greatly from those of today. But the process itself should be exemplary for all the confused folk alive in our era, if we can muster the courage to tackle it. Feminist thought can well be defined as a self-analysis of women by women, taking account of neurotic behavior and hopeful dreams too. We can't expect to be totally objective but we will have plenty of criticism from people of both genders to offset the dangers of subjectivity. At least we won't be contributing to the cancerous polarization of society by inventing a new, or reinforcing an old, "right way" of dividing and ranking human beings. The goal of this self-analysis is precisely to heal that split. To achieve that aim sets us a complex task: to imagine new ways of managing affairs that are neither those of the old oppressors, nor ones that come only from remembrance of oppression. We have to refuse a policy of deference and irresponsibility as a way of avoiding blame, and also somehow live beyond the resentment and the suppressed fury that accompanied submission as a natural response but as one that tied us to the role of female; the split and divided role of charmer and manhater both. Two polarizations are there to be healed: those in the self of both women and men, and the split that has partitioned the world into "us" and "them" for so long. One way or another we have to consent to the burdens and the delights of being fully human.

I haven't the faintest idea as to whether we will ever manage to do that, but unless we try, humanity will never have a chance to reach wholeness either.

Notes

Chapter 2

1. Douglas R. Hofstadter, *Scientific American*, February 1982, p. 20.

Chapter 4

1. Virginia Woolf, *Three Guineas* (New York: Harcourt, Brace & World, 1938), p. 61. .

Chapter 5

1. Helen Merrell Lynd, *On Shame and the Search for Identity* (New York: Harcourt, Brace and Company, 1958), p. 27.

2. Ibid. p. 35.

3. Ibid. p. 65.

4. Patricia Crawford, "Attitudes to Menstruation in Seventeenth-Century England," *Past and Present,* p. 61 (Oxford, Eng.: May 1981).

5. Ibid.

6. Mary Douglas. *Implicit Meanings: Essays in Anthropology* (London: Routledge & Kegan Paul; Boston: Henley, 1975), pp. 61–62.

Chapter 6

1. William H. Chafe, *Civilities and Civil Rights: Greensboro, North Carolina, and the Black Struggle for Equality* (New York: Oxford University Press, 1980), p. 119.

2. Eugene D. Genovese, *Roll Jordan, Roll: The World the Slaves Made* (New York: Pantheon Books, 1974), p. 4.

3. Ibid. p. 145 and n. 30, p. 702.

4. Ibid. p. 146.

5. Ibid. p. 147.

6. Rodney Needham, ed., *Right and Left: Essays on Dual Symbolic Classification* (Chicago: University of Chicago Press, 1973), passim.

Chapter 7

1. Eric Foner, *Nothing but Freedom: Emancipation and Its Legacy* (Baton Rouge: Louisiana State University Press, 1983). A discussion of the measures enumerated here runs throughout Chapter 1, most especially pp. 12–31.

2. Ibid. n. 2, p. 28.

3. Jacques Le Goff, *Time, Work and Culture in the Middle Ages,* trans. Arthur Goldhamer (Chicago: University of Chicago Press, 1980), p. 90.

4. Jerome Blum, *The End of the Old Order in Rural Europe* (Princeton: Princeton University Press, 1978), p. 45.

5. Erasmus quoted in Norbert Elias, *A History of Manners,* Vol. 1, *The Civilizing Process,* trans. Edmund Jephcott (New York: Pantheon Books, 1982), p. 18.

Chapter 8

1. Andrew Wallace-Hadrill, "The Golden Age and Sin in Augustan Ideology," *Past and Present* (Oxford, Eng.: May 1982), p. 26. (ms. page 108).

2. Ibid. p. 29.

3. Ibid. p. 29.

4. Ibid. p. 32.

5. Ibid. p. 36.

6. Michael T. Ryan, "Assimilating New Worlds in the Sixteenth and Seventeenth Centuries," *Comparative Studies in Society and History* (Cambridge, Eng.: Cambridge University Press, October 1981), p. 520.

7. Ibid. pp. 530, 531.

8. Silvano Arieti, *Interpretation of Schizophrenia,* 2nd rev. ed. (New York: Basic Books, 1974), p. 378.

Chapter 9

1. Eric Hobsbawm and Terence Ranger, eds., *The Invention of Tradition* (Cambridge, Eng.: Cambridge University Press, 1983), p. 221.

2. Ibid p. 236.

3. Ronald Blythe, *Akenfield: Portrait of an English Village* (New York: Pantheon Books, 1969), pp. 276–278.

4. Ibid.

5. Ibid. p. 55.

6. Dorothy Hartley, *Lost Country Life* (New York: Pantheon Books, 1979), pp. 185–186.

7. Blythe, op. cit. p. 130.

8. Daryl Chinn, "Letter," *Johns Hopkins Magazine* (August 1958), pp. 3–6

Chapter 10

1. Elizabeth L. Eisenstein, *The Printing Press as an Agent of Change: Communications and Cultural Transformations in Early Modern Europe* (Cambridge, Eng., and New York: Cambridge University Press, 1979).
2. "Science and the Citizen," *Scientific American* (January 1986), pp. 60, 62.

Chapter 11

1. Louise Bernikow. *Alone in America* (New York: Harper & Row, 1986), p. 13.
2. "All Things Considered," National Public Radio, December 27, 1965.
3. Benjamin R. Barber, "Voting Is Not Enough," *Atlantic Monthly* (June 1984).

Chapter 12

1. Gene Sharp, *The Politics of Nonviolent Action* (Boston: Porter Sargent, 1973), p. 657, and n. 1, p. 698.
2. H. Jon Rosenbaum and Peter C. Sederberg, eds., *Vigilante Politics* (Philadelphia: University of Pennsylvania Press, 1976), Introduction, p. 10.
3. Richard Maxwell Brown, "Vigilantism in America," in Rosenbaum and Sederberg, p. 79.
4. Dudley Clendenin, "North Carolina Jury Getting Case Against Klan Paramilitary Group," *The New York Times,* July 25, 1986.
5. "All Things Considered," National Public Radio, June 25, 1986.
6. Brown, op. cit. pp. 88–90.
7. Ibid. p. 97.

Index

INDEX